The Nimble C-Suite

How to Align the Diverse Strengths of Your Executive Team to Predictably Deliver Extraordinary Outcomes in a Transformational Economy.

D0782906

Published by NimbilityWorks Media™
NimbilityWorks.com/media

v1.01

ISBN 978-1-884059-65-0 Paperback
ISBN 978-1-884059-66-7 Hardback

Printed in the United States of America.

The Nimble C-Suite

How to Align the Diverse Strengths of Your Executive Team to Predictably Deliver Extraordinary Outcomes in a Transformational Economy.

Amid perpetual upheavals and accelerating world changes, we transition from the Experience Economy where buyers chose *memorable* outcomes to the Transformational Economy where buyers choose *meaningful,* authentic, and socially responsible outcomes.

Because your customers want to become a better version of themselves, your company must become a better version of itself.

This book's premise: the future belongs to the nimble; those able to resiliently innovate to deliver meaningful goods and services that customers seek. Being nimble makes demands beyond the traditional corporate structure and leadership strategy's ability to deliver.

This book is your essential bridge from the conventional business approaches you used to get where you are today, to flourishing in a Transformational Economy as a socially responsible business.

In it, we'll provide you with a fresh look at the root causes that limit leadership teams and offers overdue solutions that can address these causes in today's chronically volatile business environment.

Early Praise

"This is a great book filled with innovative ideas and at the same time utterly readable and digestible. Bravo. The future belongs to those who overcome the current chaos and become nimble. Gruder and Smith clearly lay out the framework that includes completely rethinking the organizational structure to maximize leadership archetypes and provide the most streamlined and reliable way to ensure psychological diversity and minimize blind spots. Each chapter ends with probing questions to help critically evaluate an organization's status and begin the journey to nimbility."

– Melissa A. Smith, former Executive Director of the **Institute for Ethical Leadership at Rutgers Business School**, and former President of Retail, **Aerosoles Inc.**

"Only once in a great while do words hold tremendous power to invoke significant change. The authors, Dr. David Gruder and Mark S.A. Smith have collaborated to create a foundation for leadership in a world where the rate of change has become so exponential that it calls for an entirely new perspective in leadership. To say that we are in a transformational phase of human evolution would be an understatement, and this set of books sets the path forward in a way never before attempted at such

a grand scale. We will include copies of these books in every HR package, not just for the executives."
– Mark Hewitt, Founder, **NuGen Development** & **The Lydian Foundation**

"Color me impressed! Here's why Dr. Gruder and Mr. Smith's book is so very valuable to devour: The future is coming and only the nimble, flexible, and innovative of us will contribute and prosper in that future. This book shows how to BE the Leader in these times because it is remarkably rich in detail and specific tactics and it truly inspires the reader to 'nimbly' take action. Powerfully important read."
– David M. Corbin, Mentor to Mentors, Two-time WSJ best-selling author, *The Illuminated Brand, Illuminate the Negative, BrandSlaughter*

"Aligning the strengths and mindset of your executive team has become critical to thriving in today's chaotic world. I have known David and Mark for many years, and they have captured in their new book what you must understand and do to predictably and successfully lead the next generation of business."
– Dr. Jeffrey Magee, CMC/CBE/CSP/PDM, Human Capital Developer, Group-Publisher & Editor-and-Chief, *PERFORMANCE* Magazine

"I truly loved the book! To the point, immediately useable information, with an amazing and necessary map for executives to step forward into the new corporate paradigm that already has me wondering how the old paradigm lasted this long!"

– Dail Croome, President, **Grand Shrimp** (decentralized food production solutions); former President & Vice President of several public & private companies

"As a successful leader of new emerging global technology businesses for 20 years, I extracted new ideas and was reminded of some I allowed to lapse. I kept going back and reading parts over again. Early in the book the authors ask: Are you willing to unlearn and relearn? This impactful statement freed me to investigate the wisdom and ideas provided without judgment. Leaders and teams will benefit immediately from this book."

– Dan Wensley, CEO, **ScalePad** (technology)

"Reading this book blew my mind! As a seasoned COO, I still face daily challenges. This book explains why, especially the chapter on executive temperament and aligning roles to operate within one's zone of genius. This is my new go-to manual for permanently solving my biggest leadership problems."

– Peter Vescovo, COO, **Island Tech Services** (technology)

"The concept of *Nimbility*, used liberally by the authors, is one of those transformative words like *grit*. If you do not recognize its tremendous impact on your business and your people, your results will suffer, and success will be as elusive as Ponce de Leon's fruitless search for the

Fountain of Youth. This book will show you how to find it and harness its power."
– Steve Minucci, Senior Vice President, **One Trusted Advisor** (financial services)

"Wow! The roadmap to understanding C-Suite mindset and temperament, *The Nimble C-Suite* lays out why each of the team makes the decisions that they do. I've been working with executives for years, running their Executive Customer Advisory Boards, and this brings into sharp focus why certain execs think the way they do. It's like having X-ray vision into their brains."
– Betsy Westhafer, CEO, **The Congruity Group** (executive services)

"The right mindset and skill set make up a dream team. Yet as a business leader for decades, I now have a whole new understanding of how people interact to make a team that makes the dream come true. Expect massive insights on how to make your dream team a powerhouse reality."
– Stormy Andrews, CEO, **Yokel Local** (marketing)

"While I oversee a small operation, even after decades of business experience, I often use the insights and systems that larger operations use to grow their people and their bottom line. While the ideas in this breakthrough book target larger teams, I've gathered several new insights that I'll use immediately to improve my operation. This is the leadership manual that I'll share with my closest colleagues, as it's compatible with my heart-centered leadership style."

– Bill Kerwood, **BillKerwood.com** (entertainment and education)

"Read this book. You will be glad you did! In it you will find clear information on how to know what kind of problems your leadership team is struggling with and strategies to create an unstoppable team, culture, and business. The book leaps past leadership jargon and convincingly prescribes new challenges and strategies to the blocks that hold back so many CEOs, boards of directors, and teams from being successful."

– Sabrina Braham M.A. PCC Executive Coach & Founder **WomensLeadershipSuccess.com** radio podcast (executive coach)

"As much as I might try to skim this book, that was hardly possible as there are so many pearls of wisdom delivered. A few examples: how to find the freedom needed to focus on what is most important to effective leadership; vision, clear communications, and culture encouraging people to speak up and bring disruption for the sake of growth. I also loved the 'Ask Yourself' sections to really reflect on the content and identify how you can apply it to your company and leadership."

– Penny Zenker, International CEO, Author, *The Productivity Zone* (executive training)

"Over the years I have read numerous books on effective leadership. I can tell you this is the real deal. It is easy to read with multiple insights on each page that are valuable and timely. You get a comprehensive vision of what real leadership is and should be. My advice is to read it with pen in hand and embrace the advice accordingly."

– Marc McNamara, CEO of **The Enablement Group,** and host of the podcast series *The Intelligent Organization* (training company)

"In the sea of business books, *The Nimble C-Suite* stands out as a master class on how effective businesses operate, why they often don't, and how to fix your business so it thrives. With this clear, readable, and relatable book, you can have your next Executive MBA before the sun goes down today."

– KC Craichy, Founder & CEO, **Living Fuel, Inc.** (health supplements)

"I've known Mark and his great insights and questions that tease the mind and curiosity. While this book is aimed at C-Suite officers, I see enormous value for sales leaders who work on strategic accounts and engage senior executives because it lays out how they think, what they find important, and how they make decisions. Reading this book through the lens of "know your customer" brings new insights in how to make customer executives successful."

– Rajesh Rao, RVP & Director, Asia Pacific & Japan, **Viavi Solutions** (test & measurement equipment)

"With uncertainty the only thing we can be certain of in today's world, Gruder and Smith take us on a different journey – one that reminds us of the true entrepreneurial spirit – being nimble. Every business owner should read this book and learn how the "new" business world works. 10 out of 10 highly recommend!"

– Kim Kleeman - **Accelerate Successfully** Business Coach & co- founder of the Inner Circle, oinnero.com (executive coaching)

"These insights and strategies are brilliant. I suggest you consider buying a copy for every executive in your organization. Mark and David are the authorities on creating essential action and clearly explain how to deliver vital value. Your vision, plans, strategies, and future success will be improved dramatically from reading and implementing what you will learn from this great book."

– Frank Candy, Founder and President, **American Speakers Bureau Corp.**

Disclaimer

Neither the authors nor the publisher assume any responsibility for errors, inaccuracies, or omissions. Any slights of people or organizations are unintentional.

This publication is not intended for use as a source of psychological, security, technical, legal, accounting, financial, or other professional advice. If you need advice concerning these matters, consult a qualified professional as this is not a substitute for professional counsel.

Neither the authors nor the publisher accept any responsibility or liability for your use of the ideas presented herein. Conversely, neither the publisher nor authors will lay claim to any profits you make based on the principles, mindsets, and tactics this book provides.

Some suggestions concerning business practices may inadvertently introduce practices deemed unlawful in certain professions, states, municipalities, countries. You should be aware of the various laws governing your business practices in your industry and in your location. While the websites referenced were personally reviewed by the authors, we can make no guarantees as to their safety. Practice safe Internet surfing with current antivirus software and a browser with robust security settings.

Foreword

The staggering complexity of human evolution is truly a remarkable story. We are strange creatures who can walk upright and possesses supersized brains. We invent tools to meet our every need and express ourselves using remarkably complex sets of symbols. We have conquered every corner of the planet and today are in the process of becoming a truly multi-planetary species.

Our modern future began with culture and civilization that formed into a network of specialists, becoming scientists, artists, engineers, and leaders. This specialization led to many discoveries and advancements that were not possible in our earlier human evolution. Yet, this specialization inadvertently created islands disconnected from each other. We see silos of trades, skills, and cultures competing over resources rather than collaborating to utilize them wisely. This scarcity-oriented strategy is unhealthy and unsustainable.

> "A PRACTICAL BLUEPRINT IS LONG OVERDUE FOR OVERHAULING BUSINESS MANAGEMENT AND COMPANY CULTURE FUNDAMENTALS."

The Nimble series of books from Dr. David Gruder and Mark S.A. Smith is just such a blueprint. They are a breathtaking leap into a future of interconnection. The

{ xv }

authors present instruction, methods, and perspectives for executives and company management that bridge the gaps between specialists in much-needed ways that are crucial to any company's success.

The Nimble C-Suite provides practical strategies for navigating fundamental differences among executives to lead to healthy outcomes, support innovation, and empower management and staff through effective communication across the five core archetypes covered in the book. Gruder and Smith guide us through examples that catalyze the shift into a Nimble Paradigm – identifying our blind spots and building on pearls of wisdom.

I view this set of books as today's missing success guide essential for your success as a business leader, executive, or manager. I would go so far as to assert that these books will serve as crucial texts to guide the evolution of business leadership in the third millennium.

I'm not speaking in hyperbole here. I created a laminated card that I now carry in my wallet. It contains seven critical skills offered in this book that are vital reminders about my role as an executive and leader. I have made these required reading for all of those in leadership roles in all my companies. And I am utilizing Gruder and Smith to ensure effective implementation.

The Nimble books are only for you if you're looking to stretch into a wiser future. Those who aren't might not agree with, or even understand, the Nimble principles it illuminates. That's okay.

> **"LIFE IS A JOURNEY, NOT A DESTINATION."**

However, suppose you're hungry for a vastly more effective way to conceptualize and actualize business in today's transformation economy? In that case, you've just found a gem that I believe you'll be as grateful to utilize as I am.

Mark Hewitt,
Co-Founder, NuGen Development &
The Lydian Foundation

Contents

The Nimble C-Suite
How to Align the Diverse Strengths of Your Executive Team to Predictably Deliver Extraordinary Outcomes in a Transformational Economy.

Chapter 1:
Why All the Business Chaos?

Raphael looked forward to meeting with his CEO coach. He always appreciated the insights and epiphanies he received from the conversation. And right now, he needed a new perspective.

While he knew he was smart, a seasoned CEO who understood his market and knew how to run a business, there always seemed to be resistance from his team to follow his leadership. They just couldn't seem to get his vision or move fast enough. His coach, Sabrina expanded his perspective for making better decisions and communicating more effectively, and then helped him through the rough patches in mastering this expanded perspective.

And, yet… this seemed bigger than anything they had faced together. The thought he tried not to think – could I, as a CEO, be hitting my limit?

Sabrina was already at the café, sipping a cup of tea in contemplation. She never seemed rushed or busy, just thoughtful and present. He waved at her, ordered black coffee, and walked over to her table.

"Hi Raphael," she smiled broadly and motioned to the seat across from her. He sat and she looked at him intensely. "How are *you*?"

He laughed uneasily, "Good but frustrated!"

"With yourself, your team, your operation, your customers? What's the source of your frustration?" she asked gently.

"All of them! I can't seem to get traction on my plans, the team is resisting critical new initiatives, my operation can't move fast enough, and my customers are getting more demanding."

"Demanding in what way?"

Raphael noticed she first focused on the customer issues. "They want our products to be more socially responsible. What happened to the old days of customers just wanting better, faster, cheaper; you know, the impossible? Now they want us to be eco-friendly, carbon neutral, cage free, green, and 100 percent recyclable. This means complete rework of our processes, working with new vendors, and changing our marketing messaging. It's a lot."

"What if you don't do that?"

"They'll chose another, more socially responsible brand. We lose market share. The investors aren't happy. I lose my job." Raphael tried not to sound like he was complaining.

Sabrina thought for a moment. "Frustration happens when you can't control what, in the past, you thought you could. What might relieve your frustration?"

Wishfully, Raphael said, "If I could push pause for a moment, I might be able to catch up. I know that's not possible."

Sabrina smiled wisely. "Business is a series of transformations. Just like kerosene lamps replaced candles, and electric light replaced kerosene, the old ways of doing business are always being replaced as the market transforms. If you can't catch up, what else might you do?"

Raphael had a flash of insight. "So, you're telling me that I need to transform, change myself, and then the team."

"A smart conclusion. What might your transformation look like?"

"I need to think about that." Raphael wasn't ready for a question that felt that big.

"Guess..." Sabrina gently urged.

"I need a new model. All the things I know don't seem to work as well as they did. Less so every day. And I need a way to bridge the company from where we are to where we need to be to make this work."

"That's an honest assessment. Is that what you want?"

Raphael quickly answered, "Yes, it is. Where do I find the new model?"

"If you didn't have me, where would you start?" Sabrina challenged.

"I think with a blank sheet of paper, writing down what I know works now, what doesn't work anymore, and look at the gaps." It had been a while since Raphael had done that exercise.

"Good, you're thinking like a seasoned leader. Like GPS navigation, you have to know where you are and where you want to go before you can give meaningful directions to your team. What would you do next?"

"I'd need some perspective to help me deeply question everything that I do now: how we set objectives, how I make decisions, how my team works with me, how we make measurable progress." Strangely, it feels good to be honest about this, Raphael thought.

"Which of those is the starting point?"

"Given that our customers want a different objective than we've been offering, I'd start there." It seems so obvious now.

"How will you know when you've got an accurate objective, one that aligns with your customers and with your vision for the company? Don't you claim that you're customer driven now?" Sabrina quired. She rarely asked two questions at a time.

"You've got me. We've been customer driven as long as it fits our business model. Even my executive team discounts customer input these days. Ah, so I need to work on tightening my culture." Raphael knew that brutal honesty was the path forward.

"Why would you tighten your culture?" Sabrina's questions were often uncomfortably close to the truth, yet, that's why Raphael valued her perspective.

"What are you telling me?"

"While you're right that culture is the starting point of a new model, we haven't talked about you. New culture must reflect the new you or it's unsustainable. How will you first change?"

"I'm stuck there." Raphael felt he was close to the root issue.

"That's natural. Your personal identity, how you view and present yourself, has brought you to this point of your career, but won't take you any further. How do you need to change the vision of your identity to bring about the changes you want your team to embrace?"

"Well, I have a track record of getting things done, attracting top talent, and making an impression on the market." Raphael knew he wasn't answering Sabrina's question.

"Do you need to change any of those characteristics?"

"No, but something is missing" he admitted.

"Ah, you've identified a blind spot; you now know that you don't know something important. May I share with you where to explore that blind spot?"

"Yes, please." Raphael felt a slight sense of relief.

"You are exceptional at designing and building systems, as reflected by your identity. What's missing is your ability to quickly adjust those systems to adapt to the new world. While sometimes it feels like it's easier to start over, you don't have that luxury. So, you're frustrated."

"That's right!"

"How often do you substantially change your business processes?"

"It used to be about every five years but recently it's been happening more often. It's painful to change processes."

"Yes, yet your upstart competition doesn't seem to have that problem. What do they know that you don't?"

"They don't have the inertia we do" he conceded.

"True, and they don't have the reputation, capitalization, and market share you do; all important non-product-based brand differentiators that they wish they had. What allows them to make rapid changes when you can't seem to?" Sabrina seemed to always be able to state the obvious that he overlooked.

"Hmmm… they don't have to deal with existing systems that don't take well to changes and they have to start with an innovation, or they couldn't compete."

"To restate what you just realized, they have resilient systems and they embrace innovation, which defines Nimbility. You have brittle systems that break under pressure or change, so not only is innovation resisted, but it's also unrewarded in your company. You, your team, and your company are not nimble. Your thought processes reflect that lack of Nimbility because your team can't be nimble, and your company can't be nimble. Your transformation is to embrace a nimble mindset, from which everything else nimble can proceed. Do you see how this can eliminate your frustration?"

Raphael realized that this brutal honesty was true. He had only paid lip service to innovation, not making it a priority. "How do I learn more about becoming nimble?"

"Here's a book you might find valuable…"

You hold in your hand that book.

The Central Idea: Nimbility

Everything you'll read and consider in this book centers on bringing *Nimbility* to your organization.

Nimbility is the combination of high resilience and high innovation that are necessary attributes for profiting from upheavals. See Figure 1.

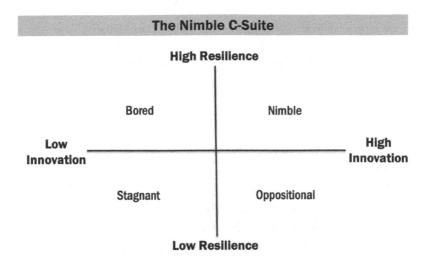

Figure 1: The Nimbility Matrix: Mapping Resilience Against
Innovation Determines Your Nimbility Level

Innovation is your capacity to increase the desirability, utility, and value of a product, whether it's goods or services. *Resilience* is your ability to recover from stress and unplanned impacts.

The obvious value of innovation is competitive performance, protecting and increasing profit margins, and corporate sustainability in a changing market. It's also way more fun. Innovation is set by culture and team rewards for looking for better ways to bring more value to the team, customers, stakeholders, and the planet.

A key value of resilience is risk reduction because it allows rapid recovery from an undesired state, reducing the cost of risk, and therefore contributing to lowered risk. Resilience is set by systems and policies that can quickly respond to change, with the necessary resources to absorb shocks and quickly recover.

> IF YOU CAN'T BOUNCE, YOU CAN'T BOUNCE BACK.
> – MARK DIMASSIMO

Nimbility is inherently lower risk, much lower than other options, making conventional risk-taking and innovation much safer from a career and corporate perspective.

We apply the Nimbility Matrix to both your organization and the individuals involved when assessing a situation. For your organization, we look at culture, systems, procedures, processes, and policies to identify how your business rules constrain or enable resilience, and limit or foster innovation. When considering individuals, we examine their behaviors as well as their attitudes and temperaments to understand their Nimbility.

Use this matrix to quickly identify your business's general level of innovation and resiliency based on your observations.

What's the Difference Between Nimbility and Agile?

The concept of an *agile organization* has been in use for quite some time, originating in the product-economy world of software to speed development. It unlocked the linear approach to product development allowing it to function iteratively with short cycles to make rapid improvements. Agile tactics are complementary to Nimbility for this purpose.

We see Nimbility as the next generation of agile, better suited for the Transformation Economy, specifically addressing management and people development strategy in a new way.

Why is Nimbility so Important Now?

Amid perpetual upheavals and accelerating world changes, you and your team are amidst transition from the *Experience Economy,* where buyers chose *memorable* outcomes, to the *Transformation Economy,* where buyers choose *meaningful,* authentic, and socially responsible outcomes.

> A MEANINGFUL EXPERIENCE IS ALWAYS HIGHLY MEMORABLE.

One could contend this started with Apple CEO, Steve Jobs, who has been described as creating a *reality distortion field.* Widely revered and criticized, there's no argument he was one of the most disruptively effective business leaders of all time.

Steve drove the transformation from personal computers being a *commodity* to becoming an *experience* that enabled creativity and innovation, and culminated in a personal device ecosystem that brought *transformation.* Transformative innovation demands reality distortion, because it brings into being a new reality not based on the existing reality. We call this Nimbility.

While Steve's competition attempted to copy his product's user experience, no company has even come close to the unified experience of Apple's offering: personal electronic devices that frictionlessly fit into one's lifestyle, interacting with each other to make life richer, easier, less stressful, and more fun. An ecosystem of computer, tablet, watch, phone, camera, TV, music device, music, applications, ear buds, speakers, data storage, locater tags and more, flawlessly interconnect and interoperate with voice and gesture, learning your preferences, making enrichening suggestions, and supporting your lifestyle. Apple products bring meaning in a memorable way to those who embrace them. A reality distortion field, indeed.

> INNOVATION DISTINGUISHES BETWEEN A LEADER AND A FOLLOWER.
> – STEVE JOBS

This distorts the reality of Apple's competitors – they can't fathom what they're experiencing because they're looking at this through the experience economy lens (purchases wrapped in something memorable) instead of the transformational economy (purchases that move to meaningful).

Memorability without meaning may be captivating but it's not helpful (cool, but not useful), unsustainable (I've already seen that), or uncompetitive (you're a copycat).

Bringing meaning to customers is now the leading edge of competitive advantage: meaning in being authentically part of community, being environmentally responsible, and being a leader in improving the human condition.

Because your customers want to become a better version of themselves, your company must become a better version of itself.

To do this requires Nimbility.

Even the military has adopted Nimbility, opting for small autonomous teams of fighters, completely self-contained and self-directed to reliably accomplish the assigned mission in the face of chaos.

The Drive to the Transformational Economy

Our planet has been through six economies producing the primary source of enterprise profits. While all of these individual economies still remain, their profit impacts lessen with the emergence of the next economy.

The key idea is that the value proposition and sales method changes with each economic wave. What works in one business model fails in the next wave. Here's a simplified overview of these economic waves.

We started when we were in tribes with the *subsistence economy*, producing enough for their needs and little more. The goal was, "I'm alive."

When tribes settled, the *commodity economy* flourished, producing agriculture, mining, timber, and other natural resources where people bought essentials. The goal was, "I'm a productive person."

The *product economy* began with the industrial revolution, where people bought labor savings. The goal was, "I'm an efficient person."

The *service economy* emerged post WW II when two-earner families needed to buy time, so purchased services (repairs, cleaning, food prep, professional services, etc.) to make up for their overworked life. The goal was, "I'm a free person."

The *experience economy* emerged in the '90s when people chose memorable experiences (social media, Netflix, Google, Yelp, Las Vegas, etc.). The goal is, "I'm an interesting person."

In the *transformational economy*, emerging in the 2018 timeframe, people buy meaningful and authentic products, services, and experiences. The goal is, "I'm a better person."

The transformation economy will be equally disruptive with the prior economies and will require new approaches to product design, marketing, sales, customer service, and business management. We'll explore these approaches in this book.

Transforming from a Scarce Mindset to an Abundant Mindset

A big mindset shift required to transition to the Transformational Economy demands consideration of seeing the world as abundant instead of scarce.

Scarcity has been a prime driver for prior economies: scarce food, scarce commodities, scarce resources, scarce time, scarce enjoyment. This has been codified by economists as seeing resources as a fixed pie, where if one takes a slice, there is less available for others.

You may recall being taught in Econ class the guns versus butter dilemma where funds were available for arms or food and leadership traded one for the other in the totality of available resources. Monopolies formed to control supply of transportation, oil, and power creating forced scarcity. Justifying a scarcity mindset forces a scarce world view.

With an abundance mindset, the pie keeps expanding, making more and more resources available. Proof of this is Moore's law, where compute power doubles roughly every 18 months, decreasing the cost of computing accordingly. Compute power is an increasing supply, not a scarcity of it.

> CHANGE IS NOT MERELY NECESSARY TO LIFE - IT IS LIFE.
> – ALVIN TOFFLER

Alvin Toffler in his seminal book, *The Third Wave*, discussed how improved technology decreased scarcity. He talked about how farming technology increases crop production, to the point where 100 years ago, more than half of the population was producing food, and now fewer than one percent does. He discussed the belief that real estate was scarce, yet we have increased real estate availability through high-rise buildings, massively compounding usable space. Real estate that was once undesirable because of climate and location have become desirable through air conditioning and Internet access, making almost any location with electrical power livable. Power is no longer scarce, because if you have wind, waves, or sunshine, you can produce power. Scarce water resources can be made abundant with commercial reverse osmosis and one can extract personal quantities of water out of the air, all that's required is power. Scarce labor can be replaced with robotics, automation, and AI. You get the point.

In the Transformational Economy, leaders experience abundance everywhere, it's just a matter of seeing it, tapping into it, and using it with integrity. Operating from this mindset opens new transformational opportunities, as the definition of transformation is to convert from one form to another, more desirable form.

The truly scarcest resource is cognitive capacity, as one has a limited number of decisions that can be made in a day. Yet even this can be bolstered by systems and self-care.

How do you see making the shift to an abundant mindset could help you resolve some of the issues you are facing?

Navigating Non-stop Upheavals

In today's topsy-turvy, chaotic world, big disasters and big opportunities seem to always be just around the corner. And you've probably noticed that they're occurring faster with more impact than ever before.

Perhaps you see one of these upheavals looming or currently unfolding in your business, and you aren't clear about the best way to utilize it. You are not alone.

> EVERY ADVERSITY, EVERY FAILURE, EVERY HEARTACHE
> CARRIES WITH IT THE SEED OF AN EQUAL OR GREATER BENEFIT.
> – NAPOLEON HILL

The toll of relentless upheavals is more unchecked stress, more disrupted careers, and more uncertainty in business, society, politics, and personal lives. So, the big question for executives in today's world is, how can you align and optimize resources to capitalize on all this chaos instead of being swallowed by it? Become nimble.

Facing Upheavals?

You see these, just as we do. Companies are collapsing under the weight of:

❑ Inflexibility, which prevents nimble navigation of chaos and forced change

❑ Upheaval-skilled leadership deficits – anti-Nimbility – which worsen the impact of upheaval

❑ Confusion about how to innovate in a rapidly changing economic, political, and cultural environment, which results in wasted time, energy, mental capacity, and other resources

❑ Uncertainty about how to train executives and teams to surf these changes, instead of being drowned by uncontrollable circumstances.

The Warring C-Suite

All of this is exacerbated by a warring C-Suite.[1] If you're like most executive leaders, you are amidst a battle with your executive team. Sure, it might be mostly quiet now, yet you know that it's just a matter of bringing up the wrong topic, a misconstrued comment, or another missed target, before the rhetoric heats up and everyone is at each other's throats, yet again.

---

[1] We define C-Suite for the purposes of this book as the executive team who are individually accountable and responsible for key business functions in the organization, traditionally recognized by the word *Chief* in their title.

In our experience, every organization experiences C-Suite conflict. It's expressed as both overt battles and covert political games. No doubt, your leadership effectiveness has been diminished by the negative impacts of this.

You've done your best to assemble a cast of all-stars, yet there's still conflict. Is it your fault?

Or maybe you've inherited a big mess from your predecessor who was well-meaning but under-trained to handle the complexity and diversity of executive leadership. The team you now lead is uncontrollable and undisciplined. Do you have to replace all of them?

Or perhaps you've inherited your position from a successful relative who has done well enough, but hasn't kept up with the times, and now the competition nips at your heels. You couldn't bear leading the demise of the family legacy, yet you can't replace your family with new blood. How do you get the un-fireable to innovate? Become Nimble.

Who Are You?

And what do you want?

A Seasoned CEO

You've been leading with some level of success for a decade or more. You're frustrated with your current situation and may be burned out. Your advisors don't have good enough answers and you need a fresh perspective. You may be hobbled by a broken business model or by your C-Suite being at war.

You need new perspective and need it now.

A New CEO

You've been tapped to lead a company and you want to do it right from the start. You've read all the prescribed leadership books, and although you find them inspirational, they're not relevant to your situation. You've also noticed that they offer conflicting advice and suggestions that don't fit your personality or identity.

You desire a leadership guide that works for you.

A Board Member

You're on a board of directors and you're concerned about the executive team's viability and sense execution risk because of this. You need new tools and insights so you are better able to spot the problems and suggest solutions. You don't want to tell them what to do, but you do want to make cogent observations and point them in a more fruitful direction.

You need better ways to put into words what you're seeing so you can have a more effective impact.

A Private Equity Investor

You've invested in a company because you see their potential. You desire to align and optimize its leadership because you want your capital investment to work hard. Your focus is predictably investing in a Triple Bottom Line business – one that balances the team, social responsibility, and profit – you try to offer them solid business guidance, and to provide M&A prep that enables you to get the returns you desire.

You need an authoritative guide to optimize the leadership and make sound, predictable executive choices.

A New Executive on the Path to CEO

You've been promoted to the C-Suite, and you have eyes on the CEO position. You see the opportunities and obstacles the company faces. You know politics will play a role in who's selected, and you want to make sure that you are on the top of the list when it's time to be promoted or recruited to be CEO. You need to understand business, executive development, and succession planning, at a whole new level, and you need a clear plan for navigating your career to your desired position as CEO.

A Founder or Owner

You launched your company, have achieved success, and now face new challenges and opportunities. As a company grows, each new level achieved brings new requirements. You need to develop your leadership skills, moving beyond being an entrepreneur, and begin to think like an executive. You must align your executive team, maximize valuation, and plan for succession, as your company grows beyond your current mindset and skillset. You know that many founders get kicked out of their leadership position as they bring on new sources of capital, and you want to avoid this happening to you.

You need a different kind of leadership development and a clearer vision of how to retain control by becoming who your business needs you to be as it grows.

A Leader of Leaders

You consider yourself a capable leader: you're an experienced, natural leader, who is well coached in continuous learning about world-class skills and attitudes. And yet you still find yourself frustrated because you can't get your team to fully back your key initiatives. What are you going to do?

We feel your pain. We ourselves are business owners, professional coaches, consultants, and human performance experts. We know it's not easy. Yet there is hope.

If you've got the upheavals under control and your team all marching in the same direction, this book isn't written for you… unless you want to explore the known and unknown factors that resulted in the business Nirvana you intuitively facilitated, so you can replicate it more deliberately in the future.

> YOUR ROLE IS TO PROVIDE THOUGHTFUL LEADERSHIP AND
> YOUR TEAM'S ROLE IS TO DELIVER THOUGHTFUL RESULTS.

If you've got to navigate the insanity, herd the cats, round up the squirrels, and keep peace between the ready-for-battle factions that make up your executive team, sit down, grab a pen, and get ready for new insight, new actions, and new ways to align the diverse strengths of your team to lead a competition busting, profit-record setting, and unstoppable organization that nimbly navigates an ongoing parade of upheavals.

Our Big Promise

Our promise: to open your eyes more fully to what it means to be nimble, to understand the value of Nimbility, and to show you a practical path on how to transform you and your executives into a world-class, high-performance, upheavals-resilient leadership team by embracing the concept of being nimble.

This book takes a fresh look at the root causes that limit leadership teams and offers solutions that can address these causes in today's chronically volatile business environment.

These factors aren't a secret per se. They're just not widely discussed or visible to most. They aren't included in most leadership courses. And they are inadvertently overlooked by most leadership teams.

Yet, once you see them, you'll never, ever forget them.

> ONCE YOU EXPERIENCE THE TRUTH, YOU CAN'T UNEXPERIENCE IT.

But we must warn you: you'll have work to do, personally and professionally, and you'll face arrows being thrown at you. You won't be popular with some of your team members, and most certainly, not all of them will make it with you.

What This Is Not

This book is not a regurgitation of leadership styles, advocating for one style over another. Most books written by successful business leaders tout their viewpoint and process validated by their successes. That's old news. We don't demean their success or their viewpoint. We only recognize that they likely haven't had to deal with the factors and scenarios that you – and the entire business world – face right now.

Why This Book Is Different

What makes this book different is our approach to developing dynamic, growing businesses in a world of chaos and upheaval through Nimbility. It's an optimized and nimble business framework that equips you and your team to become *Upheavals Literate* so you can minimize chaos and capitalize on upheavals. It reveals a new executive organizational design that aligns wisdom with business function to form the Nimble C-Suite. You'll discover the *Nimbility Temperament* that enables your team to utilize uncertainty and disruption to create the best possible business outcomes.

Written from Deep Knowledge

Dr. David Gruder, PhD (and a lot of other earned honors) is a well published psychologist (writing and contributing to more than 25 books) focusing on business lifecycle psychology, executive performance, culture architecture, and making integrity profitable. He has decades of deep experience in running businesses and nonprofits, and helping other extraordinary leaders resolve seemingly unsolvable business problems. He has delivered speeches, training programs, and consulting in eight countries on three continents.

Mark S.A. Smith is a seasoned business growth strategist with many published books, business guides, and training programs, who works with Fortune 100 companies and startups. With broad international experience, he has delivered more than 2,000 speeches in 54 countries on six continents. He has helped companies bring to market billions of dollars of disruptive technology, researched and developed dozens of business models, sales methods, and marketing strategies. Coaching many executives through business growth and challenging times, he has deep empathy for leadership and broad insight in how to develop and apply systems to deliver consistent results.

We together bring to you a blend of integrated business acumen, deep psychological wisdom, and seasoned systems thinking. And we're always expanding our thought to rapidly adapt to changing world conditions.

A Wholistic Perspective of Business Design

Most business books and consultants take a siloed approach to their work, without consciously and cohesively connecting their perspectives and advice to the entire business model. This limits the Nimbility of these resources.

We bring you a human-centered, seasoned approach to create an unstoppable team, culture, and business.

A Forward-Looking Perspective on What You Need Now

Academia tends to teach business through case studies that attempt to apply history to the future. This perspective isn't useful amidst rapidly changing business models, changing customer expectations, and market upheavals. You're facing situations that leaders have never seen before, so there aren't any case studies... yet.

> YOU CAN'T NAVIGATE A DYNAMIC MARKET
> THROUGH THE REARVIEW MIRROR.

You won't read a case study or anecdote without our presenting the underlying principles that you can apply to your business and more importantly, the context for when to use the principles or not.

We focus on predicable business growth by examining the required roles and responsibilities that support an upheavals-resilient business model, instead of forcing an outdated business model to support existing roles. This key paradigm shift is required for consistent business growth in today's environment.

A Model for Truly Implementing TBL and ESG

TBL stands for triple bottom line, considering planet, people, and profit, where all three must be highly fruitful for a business, its consumers, its vendors, its funders, and the public, to consider it a success.

ESG stands for Environmental, Social, and Governance. ESG a term for a socially responsible business that has largely replaced the terms "socially responsible business" and TBL. The *E* is environment corresponding to the *planet* part of the TBL. The *S* is social corresponding to the *people* part of the TBL. And the *G* is governance adding to the *profit* part of TBL, where funders and executives are devoted to:

❑ Generating financial profits through providing customers outstanding experiences with superior products

❑ Providing personnel with outstanding experiences with personal meaning and fulfillment via their productivity and development

❑ Providing the public with a company they view positively because it provides value to society instead of deriving profits at the cost of societal wellbeing.

Some companies choose the *B corp* designation to illustrate and validate their commitment to social good.[2]

Investors are increasingly applying these non-financial factors as part of their analysis process to identify material risks and growth opportunities, what some call Stakeholder Capitalism.

With more and more consumers considering social and environmental issues in making their buying choices, these guiding principles for vision and mission drive their decisions.

Sure, there are portions of the population that don't care, yet those that do wield clout, which is only increasing as the new generations that focus on socially responsible life choices become greater and greater percentages of consumers and employees.

If you desire to create a profitable TBL and ESG business, we can show you how to do this in a meaningful, scalable, and sustainable way.

Based on Root-Cause Analysis and Universal Principles

This is a root cause-focused approach to business excellence and success, based on sound psychological principles – understanding your team's way of thinking and aligning leadership – along with sound business principles – involving long-proven ways of structuring and managing business in ways responsive to current circumstances.

---

[2] "Certified B Corporations are businesses that meet the highest standards of verified social and environmental performance, public transparency, and legal accountability to balance profit and purpose." Bcorporation.net/about-b-corps

It focuses on deep diagnostics that enable you to discover why an issue is problematic, instead of teaching you symptoms control – attempting short-term management of specific issue instead of resolving them at the root cause level. It offers next generation strategic and tactical frameworks that build in psychological savvy each step of the way, so you don't fall into the trap of inspirational/motivational/wishful thinking.

We weave in temperament: world view and mindset dimensions required for successful execution of key business roles instead of the usual organization design approach of looking at the operational roles required without sufficiently understanding the subtle human capabilities required to excel in each role.

We also bring some new insights including discussion about shifting business models impacting markets, how to intelligently select key performance indicators for real performance enhancement, and how to catalyze rapid mindset shifts with your team.

Embraces the Required Diversity to Succeed

We discuss what's required for the diverse perspectives and strengths to come together to successfully communicate, collaborate, and innovate, routinely and consistently, without necessarily having to schedule specific innovation or brainstorming events, which often feel good but far too rarely produce tangible results.

You'll learn how to apply assessment tools in psychologically useful ways that harness the strengths of your team like never before. We fill in the blanks of how to use these tools because management style doesn't matter as much as temperament alignment with roles and responsibilities.

All of this equips you to provide authoritative governance and guidance from a broad perspective and a new platform that makes progressive, predictable business development possible, despite uncertain times.

Not Everyone Will Come Along

In our decades of experience, we've observed that, almost universally when a leader invokes necessary changes:

- One third of the team will be entrenched naysayers who insist that "This will never work – I've seen this before, and I'm not playing along," and they will have to be moved off the team
- One third will be neutral, adopting an "I'll just wait and see how this works out" attitude
- One third will be early supporters who say, "I've been waiting for this! I'm so glad because I've been thinking I'd have to go somewhere else."

> NOT EVERYONE WILL FOLLOW YOUR LEADERSHIP,
> NOR DO YOU WANT THEM TO.

The entrenched naysayers often have a political stake in the status quo. They might be about to retire so don't want to rock the boat or be part of what they perceive as a failed effort. Or they just don't want to consider change, much less deal with change.

Your work is to move addicted naysayers along as quickly as possible and engage with the supporters because they are the ones who will usher the neutral group into the supporter group. Don't wait too long to eliminate the naysayers' power, though, because they'll potentially sway the neutral into their camp, your transformational effort will fail, and you'll be replaced.

For seizing an upheaval to work, you must have your nimble plan in place and then execute it with your full focus. You should also be careful who you initially share your plans with because they may misconstrue them and become a naysayer when they might otherwise not have been. Facilitating a transformation requires complete clarity and we can show you how to do this.

Are you ready to make the personal and people changes necessary for you to transform your team?

How to Get the Most Out of This Book

Because of ongoing, nonstop business disruptions, you might be feeling burnt out, tired, or discouraged. Hang in there. We wrote this book to bring you a fresh, new, revitalizing vision that sparks authentic hope for your future.

We suggest that you first skim this book to identify relevant topics. You'll notice there aren't dense blocks of text because executives learn in short chunks. Scan through, read the headings and memes, and only stop and dig in where we spark your attention.

Then, as a colleague suggests, "Go through it in first gear." Take time to digest, debate, question, consider, adapt, and ultimately pivot your team to a new vision. If you need to discuss some of these points, contact us, and one of us, or one of our team members, will be glad to help.

Here are a few ways to get the most from your investment in reading this.

Get Ready to Unlearn and Learn

Are you willing to unlearn and relearn? This book requires you to suspend judgement so you can see the big picture we are painting, decide which specifics will be right for you, and then bring them to your team.

> THE ILLITERATE OF THE 21ST CENTURY WILL NOT BE
> THOSE WHO CANNOT READ AND WRITE,
> BUT THOSE WHO CANNOT LEARN, UNLEARN, AND RELEARN.
> – ALVIN TOFFLER

A potential blind spot for you is believing your current organizational design and business model is what will continue to work for you. We call resistance to required change *Paradigm Attachment Disorder* – the insistence that your experience, the box you're in right now that's been created by your identity and culture, will always work in the future. With the radical changes in the business world, paradigm attachment destroys the Nimbility that is required to navigate upheavals and massive changes.

Use this book to help you unlearn and learn. Underline phrases, circle paragraphs, fold down pages, make notes, note your points of opposite opinion. A pristine book doesn't work as well as one that's marked up and mutilated. Don't worry, you can get another copy for your archives.

The bad news: most of what you and your team know won't work in the future.

> "IN TIMES OF CHANGE,
> LEARNERS INHERIT THE EARTH,
> WHILE THE LEARNED FIND THEMSELVES
> BEAUTIFULLY EQUIPPED TO DEAL WITH A WORLD
> THAT NO LONGER EXISTS."
> – ERIC HOFFER

The good news: your cognitive capacity, your ability to handle complexity and figure it out from the proper perspective, will be your most valuable asset.

We are going to push you out of your comfort zone. Will you be okay with us challenging you? Are you ready to handle whatever truths you discover as you apply the principles and perspectives we provide?

> THE LEADER'S ROLE IS TO COMFORT THE AFFLICTED
> AND AFFLICT THE COMFORTABLE.

If not, save yourself some grief and put this book down.

If so, let's go!

Boldly Go Where You Haven't Been

Nimbility is being able to conceive of a future that doesn't yet exist, that you'll create using methods you haven't yet experienced nor invented.

This requires courage to focus on the strategic and objective *what* that you're going to do, and the motivational *why* that you're doing it, without yet knowing the tactical *how* that you'll get it done.

Can you allow this new vision to emerge in the face of doubt and uncertainty of how you'll get it done?

> "STORM YOUR OWN GATES OR OTHERS WILL."
> – CHRIS STARK

What to Expect

The future is a moving target and Nimbility is about surfing the chaos to create a business that is sustainable, scalable, profitable, and ultimately, saleable.

Some of what you'll read you already know… almost. We'll be challenging you to think about it in a new way.

Some of the things you'll discover, you used to do but stopped even though they were valuable. We'll remind you that it's time to do them again.

And, without a doubt, we have many new ideas for you. When you choose to use them, you'll become as successful as you wish.

Are you ready for the transformation?

A Final Note on Our Writing Style

You may notice some intentional minor repetition as you read. This is because we want skimming readers to get the idea in context without having to read this book from beginning to end.

When we use *or* in a list of options, assume that it's an *inclusive or*, meaning the list could be *and, or,* or *all* items listed. This keeps us from using the clumsy *and/or* reference. If it's any different, we'll be explicit in our writing.

Chapter Summary

❑ Disruptive forces rock traditional business models and threaten your livelihood.

❑ Responding well to these disruptions counterintuitively requires you to change leadership and business models, embracing Nimbility to go from surviving to thriving.

❑ Changing leadership models requires your willingness as a business executive to become nimble and explore strategies and tactics that haven't been used before.

Ask Yourself

❑ What have I noticed about the disruptions my business is facing and the changes my business is faced with making?

❑ How is our lack of Nimbility impacting our present and future?

❑ How could becoming nimble create a better path to future success?

❑ Am I willing to invest time and energy to uplevel my leadership so we can exploit the new business realities?

Ask Your Team

❑ What changes do we need to make to be more relevant to our customers and become more valuable to our target market?

❑ What would it be worth for us to do that?

❑ What would it cost if we didn't do that?

Action Plan

☐ Keep reading.

☐ Mark up this book, take notes, bend over pages.

☐ Determine who else needs to read this. Buy them a copy and have them debate the concepts with you and each other.

Chapter 2:
Resolving the Battle of the Executives

As we move beyond the causes of upheavals and some of the new impacts that you and your team must address, let's explore what may prevent them from being most resourceful in addressing chronic chaos.

Let's dig into root causes of C-Suite conflict to identify where you would be wise to put some thought and effort. We discuss remedies later in the book.

The Over-functioning Board Versus the Over-Functioning CEO

Over-functioning happens when someone's neglect or under-performance is compensated for by another who tries to be the hero by filling that gap.

> "IF I DON'T DO IT, WHO WILL?" INDICATES A HERO CULTURE
> THAT IS UNSUSTAINABLE AND BRITTLE.

We see two common top-level hero situations:
- ☐ The board of directors completely drives the organization instead of allowing the C-Suite to do its job.

This is frequently the case in family-owned businesses where the founder assumes the role of Board Chair but continues to direct the company as if they were still in active leadership. This stifles innovation, paralyzes the executive team, and teaches them to under-perform.

❑ The CEO completely drives the business without utilizing the sage wisdom, governance, and guidance of a well-functioning board. This over-functioning frequently occurs when a founder hasn't brought on a true board of directors. The result is a business that's ripe for upheaval, and in the case of a publicly traded company, a hostile takeover. We discuss this situation later in this book.

In both versions of top-level over-functioning, the executive team lacks true leadership and ends up fending for themselves, or there is a revolving door of top leadership and critical talent.

Business Function Silos Kill Innovation

A business function silo develops when responsibilities – such as product development, marketing, sales, credit, and legal – operate with little attention to their impact on, or the impact of, other business functions. Silos essentially act like outsourced services to the rest of the organization instead of co-creating the synergy that is necessary for optimal operation and true Nimbility. Silos stifle flexibility, co-innovation, and cooperation.

> NOTHING KILLS "ONE TEAM – ONE GOAL" THINKING LIKE SILOS.
> – JOHN G MILLER

Silos form when departments operate independently of the rest of the organization. This often occurs when top management abdicates responsibility to a functional department head, or a department self-isolates in an attempt to insulate their performance from a dysfunctional leader.

Silos are warning signals of an impending upheaval because critical information stops flowing in both directions, and this forms massive blind spots in that department and in the executive team.

Conflicts over Role Lens Differences

Every business function and role requires a specific world view, which we call a *lens*. If the lens being used doesn't match what the role requires, the team leader makes inadvertent mistakes and exhibits poor judgment. Each executive role demands different lens components, which have to do with mindset, skillset, and toolset. The combination of diverse executive lenses is what brings the best blend of stability and innovation to an organization.

> WHERE WE ALL THINK ALIKE, WE DON'T THINK MUCH.
> – ROBERT CIALDINI

When an executive team misinterprets each other's lenses, or doesn't understand the necessity of multiple lenses, a high degree of distrust develops that sometimes deteriorates into downright hatred. Executives with differing lenses start being viewed as the enemy instead of embracing and leveraging the diverse richness and necessary perspective each lens brings to a healthy business.

We'll dig into the required and desired lenses for each executive role in this book. We'll also show you how to look at right-talent lens placement and how to avoid trust-busting team misunderstandings.

Confusion of Strategic and Tactical Roles

Strategy is a longer-range context for manifesting a company's vision and mission. Strategy defines *intention*: the aim, goal, and desired outcome. Strategic executive roles are responsible for answers to the questions about *what* is to be accomplished and avoided – the key outcomes – and for the company's big *why* question – what, exactly, is our motivation for doing this?

At the strategy level, we don't initially need to know *how* this gets accomplished. Strategy requires a longer view of the future, where much is unknown and yet to be innovated, invented, or discovered. A specific mindset is required to foresee and work with the unknown, and to plot a profitable path toward the uncertain.

> IN A NIMBLE ORGANIZATION, STRATEGY ALWAYS PROCEEDS TACTICS, BECAUSE STRATEGY BASED SOLELY ON KNOWN TACTICS KILLS INNOVATION.

Without broad alignment of the strategic *what* (mission) with the *why* (purpose) across your organization, energy gets squandered by well-meaning team members working at cross purpose, with the wrong focus, or through misunderstanding the objective.

Tactical roles are essential to execute the strategy. They fulfill the requirements of business functions that are necessary to operate a sustainable, scalable, profitable, and salable business (in the stock market or to private investors). Tactical roles take care of the *sequence* to accomplish the mission: *when* tasks happen, and *where* they happen, and the *tactical* implementation: *who* performs the tasks, *how* the work gets done, and the *resources* that are needed to get the work done.

Not all essential roles are strategic. For example, accounts payable is tactical, yet essential. The sales function is tactical, yet essential. Not all essential roles are tactical. The chief executive officer is strategic and essential, as there can only be one chief architect for a business.

> AS TOO MANY CHEFS SPOIL THE SOUP,
> TOO MANY CHIEFS SPOIL THE STRATEGY.

Why You Can't Mix Strategic and Tactical Roles

Tactical role lenses are quite different from strategic role lenses. When one person fills both a strategic and tactical role, they must use a high degree of awareness to separate the very different thought processes and lenses that each role requires. In larger organizations, this is almost impossible, as many leaders have a specific identity, both personal and corporate, that consciously or unconsciously prevents them from successfully shifting between roles or blocks their ability to innovate in the face of uncertainty.

> A MINDSET SHIFT REQUIRES A SHIFT IN IDENTITY.

We've frequently seen this happen with Chief Revenue Officers who have either a strong marketing focus or a complete sales focus at the cost of the other, and in Chief Human Resource Officers who have a strong policy enforcement mentality (this undermines their ability to keep top, innovative talent), that overrides their need to focus on critical human potential development (they lag in their ability to attract and develop top talent).

Clayton Christensen in his classic book, *The Innovator's Dilemma* documents in detail the failure of top companies to remain competitive. We see the root cause of this as the inability of initially successful leaders to retain the Nimbility that resulted in their earlier success. They either can't role switch, or they get stuck with the tactical deployment model they originally developed, which breaks their innovation capacity.

Why Blending Strategic and Tactical Teams Causes Confusion

Confusion about strategy, sequencing, and tactics clouds the decision-making process on executive teams. This confusion can cause them to incorrectly view a tactical decision as strategic and vice versa. This confusion harms long-term and short-term outcomes.

When a team only considers known or available tactics when making strategic decisions, they limit innovation and Nimbility. This is the tail wagging the dog.

When a team focuses on what they want to accomplish, they'll discover or innovate new ways to achieve their desired outcome. This generates new value, a strong competitive advantage, and greatly enhanced ability to nimbly navigate upheavals.

For example, all tech unicorns (new companies valued at $1 billion or more) bring clear innovation to market instead of recycling established tactics. They do this by starting with a blank whiteboard in a room full of unconstrained, nimble thinkers. They don't ask, "What do we *know how* to do?" They ask, "What do we *want* to do?" Then they hand off the "How do we do that?" question to their tactical teams to figure out and implement.

> NIMBLE LEADERS CREATE A FUTURE THAT DOESN'T YET EXIST,
> USING METHODS THAT HAVEN'T YET BEEN INVENTED,
> WHERE BEST PRACTICES HAVEN'T YET BEEN ESTABLISHED.

While it is vital for responsible strategists to provide their tactical teams with guidance, strategy refinement, and sequence intelligence, tactical teams need to rely on their tactical experts to synergistically create new outcomes.

Individuals on tactical teams often don't have the context, training, experience, or long-range mindset that are required to validate strategic decisions outside of their area of expertise. When they are nonetheless saddled with doing this, it almost always creates unnecessary resistance and dissent – avoidable upheavals.

A solution is to discerningly segment and train your team on strategy, sequence, and tactics so they clearly understand the purpose, functions, and correct applications of each of these critical management thought processes.

Later in this book, we'll discuss how to re-group your leadership teams to maximize Nimbility.

What About Transparency?

Transparency is the notion of sharing the inner workings with the team, perhaps also with customers and the rest of the world.

We see this as being a context question. What is the purpose of transparency versus obscurity? Is it to create trust versus hide information that would destroy trust? If one chooses disclosure, how much is too little or much?

Our view: there is certain information that needs to remain private, including details of long-term plans that could change, trade secrets, and certain personal information. And there is certain information that needs to be shared, such as the rationale for a decision, direction, or change. If it supports better understanding of the company's vision and mission, then share it. If it confuses those without the rest of the context, keep it tacit until the timing is right to disclose. If it's damaging, take action to fix the problem.

Reserve the "Chief" Title for Essential Roles

We see an increasing trend for organizations to invent C titles for non-essential roles. For example, Chief Joy Officer, Chief Evangelist, and Chief Inspiration Officer.

While you get to call members of your team anything you want, we advise against doing this with your team because conflating essential officers with nonessential roles turns the meaning of C-Suite into "Confused Suite."

Dysfunctional Inertia Limits Nimbility

"We've always done it that way" or "We've tried that, and it didn't work" indicates dysfunctional inertia and results in harmful rigidity during upheavals.

Inertia was defined in physics by Sir Isaac Newton in his First Law of Motion: an object at rest will stay at rest, and an object in motion will stay in motion, unless acted on by an external force.

Applied to business, a cultural position, idea, system, process, or viewpoint will continue unchanged unless acted on by management or other forces. This inertia causes blind spots that limit the range of options that your team can consider.

> OUR UNWILLINGNESS TO HEAR OUTSIDE OUR OWN ECHO CHAMBERS
> HAS SEVERELY LIMITED OUR ABILITY TO INNOVATE SOLUTIONS.
> – MAAJID NAWAZ

The positive side of corporate inertia is stability and consistency. However, these positives during stable times end up causing stress during upheavals because what once worked no longer does… much to the confusion of the team.

Often, beliefs that were once true, are no longer, because new information, new technology, new resources, new market demands, new business models, and other internal and external changes have rendered those beliefs obsolete – either no longer true or no longer useful.

Countering dysfunctional forms of inertia demands safely questioning cherished beliefs, especially those that are based on history, legacy, older technology, prior business models, and prior success.

The Linchpin Change: Becoming Nimble

Navigating upheaval requires the ability to rapidly consider varying perspectives, identify the new path to positive outcomes, rapidly align your team to that path, and then pursue the path in ways that eliminate execution risk and unsupportive inertia. We call this *executive Nimbility*, and we view this as a linchpin skill in becoming *upheavals literate*.

Nimbility Deficits That Impact Desired Outcomes

During an upheaval, exaggerated fear can magnify and accelerate it, when what is needed is bringing your team into an optimal psychological state for harnessing the chaos. Let's explore team Nimbility deficits that drive executive battles and block the necessary Nimbility for thriving through upheavals.

Paradigm Attachment Disorder

One's identity creates a box in which we live. When you remain committed to your box by refusing to recognize that it is no longer useful or resourceful, you've got *Paradigm Attachment Disorder* (PAD). This attachment can happen because of nostalgia, wishing for a past situation, attempting to repeat an unrepeatable peak experience, or holding on to a cherished memory.

One of the saddest versions of this is when someone believes that high school was the best years of their life. We'll bet you know someone like that. We sure do.

Stuck Identity

Most of all, Paradigm Attachment happens when we have unintentionally built our sense of identity so tightly around a specific worldview and selfview that any threat to it feels like an attack on the essence of who believe we are.

Telling War Stories

You can detect PAD when team members insist on wistfully telling old stories about how things used to be rather than working on envisioning and creating the future, or when they keep supporting traditional business models or entrenched *best practices* despite market demands for innovation. Counterintuitively, best practices can stifle innovation and limit Nimbility.

> BEST PRACTICES ARE A MOVING TARGET.

"Yes, But..."

You can also detect PAD when a team member repeatedly responds to ideas with, "Yes, but…" Anyone can have that reaction from time to time, yet when this is a pattern, it indicates addiction to the status quo.

If you've ever taken improv classes, you'll recall that the first thing you learned was that "Yes, but…" stops the flow while "Yes, and…" keeps the scene in play. The same is true in business. Start fostering a corporate culture of, "Yes, and…" in place of "Yes, but…"

> LET TRADITION BE YOUR INSPIRATION, NOT YOUR ANCHOR.

Here is an example of how to get past PAD. Celebrate the past because it got you to this point. Memorialize wisdom about principles to bring forward and what to not repeat. Then move forward by identifying new resourceful or upgraded principles that can fuel the future, while letting go of no-longer-resourceful principles that would tether you to the past.

The Broken Leadership Model Paradigm

A popular notion is that leadership styles drive success. For instance, one current view is that servant leadership is highly desirable, and this approach has acquired many fervent followers who are quite attached to this identity. Yet if you chose this style for all situations, you'll invite unnecessary upheaval. Surprised? Read on.

Singularly focusing on leadership style can be more a hinderance than a help in a nimble organization. Each style can produce certain results at the expense of overlooking critical issues. A leadership style's effectiveness depends highly on context and objective, which is a moving target in today's chaotic market. Your favorite leader's book probably discusses leadership in a world that no longer exists.

Blindly leaning on a particular leadership style (*Paradigm Attachment Disorder)* can unwittingly produce more upheavals than it solves. In addition, if your team has conflicting leadership styles, this can create massive, unnecessary conflict as each insists that their style – attached to their personal identity – is the best.

For your review, here's a list of ten of the most widely recognized leadership styles, each with an example and characteristics, and presented from least directive (collaborative) to most directive (dictatorial).

Servant (Supportive)

Mother Teresa. People-first mindset, gaining results from a personally fulfilled team, helpful. Culturally based, freeform collaboration, personal satisfaction, and mutual respect. Works best with some nonprofits, religious, and volunteer organizations.

Hands Off (Laissez-Faire or Free Thinking)

Absent parent. Focuses on personal tasks and delegating everything possible. Directs team members with limited supervision. Useful with highly experienced teams and clear, unchanging objectives.

Visionary (Charismatic)

Steve Jobs, CEO, Apple. Drives change through inspiration and influence. Works well with a seasoned team. Useful for fast growing and restructuring organizations.

Democratic (Participative)

Jeff Bezos, CEO, Amazon. Considers team input before making decisions, equal participation. Creates high levels of team satisfaction and involvement. Works best in innovative and creative industries.

Coach

Most sport team coaches. Sets clear goals, provides feedback. Balances the needs of the company with the needs of the team members. Can be time intensive.

Pacesetter

Jack Welch, CEO, GE. Drives fast results and better performance. Sets high standards and demands accountability. Works best with motivated teams and fast-moving markets.

Transformational (Structural)

Herb Kelleher, CEO, Southwest Airlines. Coaching with a focus on organization objectives and remote teams. Blends delegation and coaching. Works best with experienced teams and clear, unchanging objectives.

Transactional

Bill Gates, CEO, Microsoft. Performance focused, highly structured. Uses incentives (bonuses) and punishment (demotion). Works to hit revenue goals, often at the expense of limiting innovation.

Autocratic (Authoritarian)

Military General. Focused on results and efficiency, in control. Gives orders and expects them to be followed. Useful with inexperienced teams that require little creativity or strike forces that must instantly follow orders without question in urgent life-and-death situations.

Bureaucratic

Colin Powell. Guided by rules and procedures, with defined penalties for non-compliance. Works in highly regulated situations.

To put these leadership styles into perspective, Figure 2 illustrates a constellation of these styles when considering a talent focus versus systems focus spectrum against company goals versus team goals spectrum.

Figure 2: Comparing Leadership Styles against Leadership Goals and Operational Focus

To provide a different perspective, Figure 3 illustrates a constellation of these styles when considering a tactical, task-based focus versus a strategic, intention-based focus spectrum against the execution horizon spectrum, whether short- or long-term.

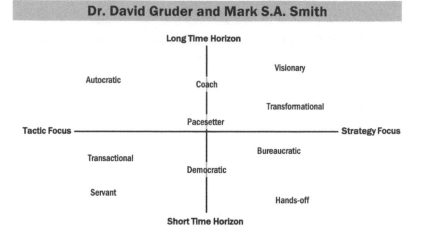

Figure 3: Comparing Leadership Styles against the Strategy versus Tactics Spectrum and Execution Time Horizons

These two ways of sorting leadership styles provide you with valuable clarity about how over-attachment to a specific leadership style can limit your options, especially when in the midst of upheavals. It also illustrates the reason for problems when your team has leadership style attachments that conflict.

A nimble executive chooses the necessary temperament required for the task at hand instead of favoring one leadership style for all situations. We go into depth on what this is and how it works in later chapters.

The Myth of the Invincible C-Suite

"They are seasoned executives; they know what to do next." Such is the myth of the invincible C-Suite. Everyone who has interacted with, been part of, or consulted to executives knows that C-Suites make many mistakes. Effective C-Suites are the ones that quickly recognize the problem and know how to quickly course correct.

When a C-Suite views themselves as invincible, they leave themselves wide open to upheavals such as business performance that goes from record breaking sales to embarrassing setbacks and hostile takeovers.

For example, a division of a market-leading test and measurement company went from market leader to negative revenue when they ignored pending legislation that when passed, would make their products unviable. After the legislation became law, their customers forced them to take back products because these didn't meet the new mandates. The company had to go through a full R&D and manufacturing cycle before they realized any new revenue.

Bringing emotional intelligence and humility to the C-Suite is the rapid cure for narcissistic, arrogant, and egotistical behaviors that invite and amplify upheavals.

> TRUE HUMILITY IS NOT THINKING LESS OF YOURSELF;
> IT IS THINKING OF YOURSELF LESS.
> – C.S. LEWIS

This requires personal growth, executive coaching, and a culture that demands focus on serving customers and won't tolerate self-serving behaviors.

Fighting Each Other Instead of Making the Competition Irrelevant

When a C-Suite becomes siloed and isolated from customers, market dynamics, and team feedback, they lose touch with the insight they need to make wise strategic decisions. They stop knowing how customers choose to spend their money and attention, and what motivates personnel to go above and beyond minimum standards.

> THE NIMBLE CEO'S JOB IS TO DIRECT THE COMPANY TO WHERE CUSTOMERS WILL SPEND MONEY IN THE FUTURE.

A siloed company or C-Suite executives who are competing against each other can rapidly overtake an organization. They stop focusing on their true role and responsibility, which is satisfying the customer today and in the future, in a short-sighted attempt to preserve or further their career.

Or worse, a corporate raider steps in and wrenches away the board of directors and replaces the executive team because of underperformance compared to their market competitors. We have seen this ugly situation play out all too frequently when an executive team gets stuck in turf wars instead of continuously upleveling their performance and focusing on the market.

Internal Politics Take Down Even the Largest Companies

Internal politics, jockeying for power, and playing dirty tricks on perceived internal enemies, all poison the synergistic collaboration demanded by today's fast-moving market.

Think about major players who have perished because of C-Suite politics. Once household name brands no longer exist because they were fighting internal battles instead of paying attention to market upheavals.

> CORPORATE POLITICS MIGHT SEEM SMART,
> BUT THEY KILL THE WILL TO SERVE CUSTOMERS.

A few that come to mind: Kodak, Polaroid, Pan American, Enron, Borders, Woolworth, Toys R Us, Digital Computer, Oldsmobile, Circuit City, Pier 1, and of course Blockbuster.

While each of these companies published a noble-sounding story about their demise, it was ultimately dysfunctional internal politics that blinded them to the upheavals that would cause them to perish.

Politics hamper effective executive consensus-based decision making. While consensus is a lovely management principle, it is rarely accomplished during upheavals without a full-cooperation culture, powerful collaboration tools, and willingness to take direction from wise counsel.

> IN A RAPIDLY CHANGING WORLD, IT'S NOT ABOUT CONSENSUS
> BUT ABOUT MAKING DECISIONS IN THE ABSENCE OF CERTAINTY,
> BECAUSE BY THE TIME YOU'VE FINALLY GAINED AGREEMENT,
> THE OBJECTIVE HAS ALREADY CHANGED.

Immaturity of Incoming Executives

You probably have noticed a distinct lack of traditional leadership skills, executive decorum, and social skills in the younger generations.

Perhaps they've been undertrained and overcoddled. They often naively expect rapid advancement as modeled in TV programs and movies and touted on social media. While they tend to be highly proficient with technology, it also rules, and arguably narrows, their social life. They rapidly switch companies, enabled by remote work expectations and a demand for a company culture that supports their lifestyle, identity, and worldview.

You can bemoan this or you can accept responsibility for providing them with training and mentoring that fills in their mindset and skillset gaps. You'll need to spell these out, along with a performance-based career path, or you can be confident that they won't stay with you long.

Neglecting this drives more upheaval as you'll be constantly hampered by a revolving door of top talent... unless you develop a comprehensive and always evolving strategy for developing and keeping the team you require and desire. We'll lay out a plan for doing this in the next chapter.

The Broken C-Suite Paradigm

Amidst continuous upheaval, the time-honored C-Suite structure has unwittingly become part of the problem.

A typical C-Suite has evolved from what should be a lean, synergistic team with a single strategic focus, to a scattered, unaligned, and tempestuous mess. Some of this mess is because of legacy business models that have outlived their usefulness, such as the Chief Information Officer reporting to the Chief Financial Officer. (This is a leftover from when computer systems were used primarily for accounting.) And some of this mess is because tactical roles have been incorporated into C-Suites, such as a Chief Human Resources Officer.

> A MISALIGNED C-SUITE
> HAMPERS NIMBILITY AND CORPORATE PERFORMANCE.

In the next chapter we will reveal a far more psychologically savvy and nimble C-Suite paradigm. One that differentiates between strategic and tactical officers in ways that make both groups far more effective. We will introduce the concept of the S-Suite (strategic suite officers) and T-Suite (tactical suite officers). You will see how even though both suites have equal importance, each has very different requirements in how they envision, plan, sequence, set timetables, execute, and oversee accountability.

By reorganizing executives in this way you're about to discover, you will vastly uplevel the Nimbility and upheavals resilience of your entire executive team like never before. Each suite will function with optimum performance, and both suites will far more deeply appreciate each suites' profound contributions to company success.

Chapter Summary

❑ The battle in the C-Suite has clearly identifiable causes. Whether it's over functioning, siloing, or politics, the CEO must lead the way to resolution and a nimbler organization.

❑ Confusion about strategic and tactical roles, each requiring a specific lens, and mixing them on leadership teams limits Nimbility.

❑ Dysfunctional inertia, where past decisions keep driving future decisions, stifles innovation and limits Nimbility, creating massive openings for upheaval.

❑ Paradigm Attachment Disorder, where one gets stuck in a non-resourceful identity, prevents Nimbility.

❑ The Myth of the Invincible C-Suite drives arrogant ignoring of current reality, increases political infighting, and distracts from the company mission, increasing the probability for upheavals.

❑ Being attached to a specific leadership style stifles Nimbility and can cause unintended negative outcomes.

Ask Yourself

❑ Do I have an over functioning board or C-Suite, where we have heroes instead of leaders? What is the impact on my team's innovation and Nimbility?

❑ Where have silos developed that limit communication, collaboration, and innovation? How does this impact my company's Nimbility?

❑ How well do my strategic leaders and tactical leaders work together? What friction results from them being on the same functional leadership team? How could splitting them into strategic (forward looking) and tactical (operational) teams improve collaboration?

❑ What dysfunctional inertia exists in my company? Where are we doing things because it's the way we've always done it?

❑ Where do we have Paradigm Attachment Disorder? Where do we have stuck identities? Who is still telling old war stories? Who routinely says, "Yes, but…?" Do I routinely say, "Yes, but…?"

❑ Do we have a culture of the Invincible C-Suite? What friction am I experiencing because we are blinded by arrogance to important insights?

❑ How is politics killing our Nimbility? What would it be worth to change this?

❑ Do I have an unhealthy attachment to a specific leadership style? If so, how is this inflexibility causing me unnecessary challenges?

Ask Your Team

❑ Do we have people on our team who routinely must take heroic measures to get the job done? How does this impact our sustainability?

❑ Where do you see silos that limit your ability to communication, collaborate, and innovate? What's the impact of this on our business?

❑ What frustrates you about your executive colleagues? Could it be their inability to see the future or to see the reality that limits us?

❑ Where in our company are we doing things because that's the way we've always done it? What's the impact of this on our ability to innovate and adapt?

❑ Where do you see us looking in the rear-view mirror instead of out the windshield at our business, where we're stuck in the past, which keeps us from moving into the future?

❑ How often do you hear, "Yes, but…" when discussing change and innovation? How do you respond to that?

❑ Do you experience our C-Suite as acting invincible, unable to even consider that it may be making a mistake? What impact does that have on our business?

❑ Do you identify with a specific leadership style? Is that style supportive in our current situation or could a more flexible approach be more effective?

❑ How much does internal politics drive our business on a scale from one to five, where one is no impact and five is high impact? What is the impact on the ability for us to change and innovate?

Action Plan

❑ Carefully consider the answers to these questions and assess the current state of the company.

❑ Consider what might be possible if these limiting issues were addressed and corrected.

❑ Without needing to know exactly how to accomplish this, prioritize the changes you need to make in yourself and then in your team that will result in measurable improvements.

❑ Keep reading to discover more ways to resolve these issues.

Chapter 3:
The Nimble C-Suite

As discussed in prior chapters, never before have businesses faced the issues that you face today. New challenges require new strategies, new structures, and new leadership thought processes. To become nimble, business leadership must go beyond business acumen.

Consider these two key skills that have until recently been missing in many executives:

❑ *Psychological Savvy* – the deep understanding of human nature that elevates personnel engagement, collaboration effectiveness, customer experience, and upheavals resilience.

❑ *Upleveled Mindset* – the world view and thought processes that keep up with the never-before-seen demands of the emerging Transformation Economy.

As you're about to discover, these two factors spell the end of the C-Suite as it has been deployed until now.

In this chapter, we lay out the first psychologically savvy construction of the executive suite. You'll see how this makes it possible to utilize the innate talent of top executives in a new, more resourceful way, while preventing burnout and bad decisions.

Introducing a New Executive Organization Model to Massively Elevate Executive Nimbility

This framework we're about to describe works for all types of corporate deployment: local, regional, or global, onsite only, virtual only, or a hybrid. It works for public, private, family-based, nonprofit, and government organizations.

It aligns cognitive capacity with roles and responsibilities, so confusion created by mental mode switching is reduced and everyone operates within their respective zone of genius.

It ensures that decisions get made in the correct order: Strategy, then Sequence, then Tactics, then Implementation. This eliminates false starts and reduces aborted missions.

It separates strategic and tactical executives into their own equally important executive suite: the strategic suite (S-Suite) and the tactical suite (T-Suite) that together make up the new nimble C-Suite.

It simplifies the Strategic Executive team (S-Suite) into only five roles.

It more fully recognizes the importance of *Implementors* who are responsible for handling the nitty gritty details.

Authentically Embrace Social Responsibility

This new structure makes it far easier than ever to implement TBL (Triple Bottom Line) and ESG (Environment, Social, Governance) and B-corp corporate philosophies. We discussed these in more detail on page 23.

It does this by creating a strategic officer whose responsibility focuses on coordinating the implementation and sustenance of TBL and ESG, ensuring these initiatives are more than just window dressing. If you're choosing TBL and ESG, or a B-corp, this new officer will substantially contribute to your success through a healthier bottom line, clearly illustrated commitment to the common good, and customer and community recognition of your company walking the talk.

> IF YOUR ENTIRE COMPANY DOESN'T WALK THE TALK,
> YOUR CUSTOMERS WILL REJECT YOUR CLAIMS
> OF BEING SOCIALLY RESPONSIBLE.

As you're undoubtedly figuring out, this chapter challenges your thinking because you're about to immerse yourself in a radical departure from traditional corporate leadership structures.

Warning: if you see the wisdom in what we present, bringing it into your company will activate resistance from some and "what took you so long" gratitude from others. Proceed when you are personally prepared with a well thought out plan.

The Biggest Blind Spot That Impairs Most C-Suites

Chances are just this side of inevitable that your C-Suite falls far shorter of its potential than you realize.

When we are brought in to help elevate C-Suite functioning, we almost always find the C-Suite is a Confused Suite comprised of impressively talented executives mixed with prematurely or inappropriately promoted budding executives. They are largely gridlocked because of unwitting misalignments between their perspective and talents, and their role and responsibility.

We find damage from nepotism and insufficiently developed talent, confusion about roles and responsibilities, an imbalance between task priority and time spent executing, and a general lack of deep understanding about the differences between strategy, sequencing, and tactics.

Why the Executive Power Struggles?

Even if your C-Suite consulted with a typical organizational development psychologist while determining your best structure, it's highly likely that your executives are still in a perpetual low-level – or even high-level – power struggle over whose perspective rules decision-making.

Unbeknownst to most executives, the secret source of these power struggles is *Archetypal Blindness*. This comes from the widespread lack of awareness of the deep impact of human archetypes on world view and decision making. As you read on, you'll discover:

❑ What archetypes are and how they influence Nimbility and outcomes

❑ The five core archetypal lenses that nimble businesses need in their S-Suite (Strategy Suite)

❑ How this realignment strengthens S-Suite collaboration to reduce blind spots, deliver extraordinary outcomes, and make it possible for you to keep thiving during upheavals.

What are Archetypes and Why Do They Matter?

Archetypes describe universal human strengths, lenses, and preferences in commonsense ways. Think of archetypes as templates for key aspects of humanness in both individuals and groups. They allow us to quickly understand what we might expect from someone of a specific archetype. We humans tend to identify more strongly with some archetypes than others.

Archetypal wisdom was originally harnessed in service of psychological development by the great psychological pioneer Carl Jung.

Some of the world's greatest novelists and scriptwriters have used this archetypal wisdom to create their most memorable characters. Examples of modern classics include George Lucas's *Star Wars*, JK Rowling's *Harry Potter*, and JRR Tolkien's *Lord of the Rings*. All have developed stories around characters with clearly identifiable archetypes with which audiences instinctively align and willing cheer on.

However, the immense value of archetypal thinking is by no means limited to psychological wellbeing and fiction writing. It is just as valuable to executive development and business thrival, as you are about to discover.

The Five Core Archetypes

The world of archetypes can appear overwhelming because of the hundreds of different versions that have been described since first introduced by Jung. However, in the early 2000s, Dr. Gruder found, and his graduate students verified, that all those can be distilled down to five core archetypes of humanness: *beingness, doingness, stability, change,* and *choicemaking.*

All others in the vast archetypal compendium are either specialized versions of the core archetypes, developmental predecessors, hybrids of two or more core archetypes, or shadow (dysfunctional) expressions of core archetypes.

Beingness is about presencing oneself – the persistent awareness of shared humanity – given an archetypal name of the *Lover*, the agape[3] form of love.

Doingness is about taking action, given an archetypal name of the *Warrior*.

Stability is about preserving predictability and standards, given an archetypal name of the *Steward*.

Change is about evolving and transforming, given an archetypal name of the *Magician*.

Choicemaking is our decisions about utilizing beingness, doingness, stability, and change to actualize our purpose (mission) in service to whatever we view as Higher Wisdom (God, Source, the Universe, etc.), given an archetypal name of the *Sovereign* (King or Queen).

These five core archetypal qualities divide into two sets of counterbalancing energies, with the fifth archetype, the Choicemaker orchestrating their use. These counterbalances are as influential in our personal lives as our work lives and they impact us as individuals and in all groups we're part of, including your C-Suite and your business.

As you see in the following diagram, beingness and doingness are natural counterbalances, as are stability and change, with the choicemaker mediating these four archetypal energies in service to the mission. See Figure 4.

---

[3] *Agape* is a Greco-Christian term referring to unconditional love, the highest form of love and charity, and the love between a Higher Power and humanity.

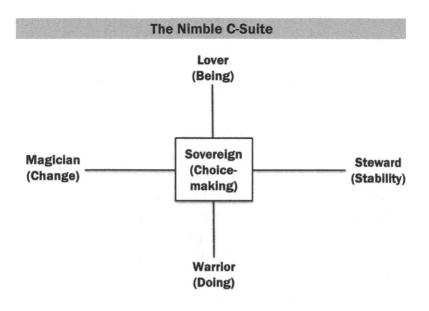

Figure 4: How the Five Core Archetypes Counterbalance and Interact

Shadow Expressions of Each Core Archetype Causes Problems

The shadow of an archetype shows up when it is over-energized at the expense of the counterbalancing archetype, which in turn tends to be under-energized. The shadow aspect produces temporary results, which is why it may be attractive, along with undesirable outcomes, which is why it's unsustainable.

For example, when there is too much beingness relative to doingness, unreliability sets in. When there is too much doingness relative to beingness, workaholism sets in. When there is too much change relative to stability, chaos sets in. When there is too much stability relative to change, stagnation sets in. Where choicemaking is driven by the wishes of the choicemaker without considering the wisdom of their team, narcissistic tyranny sets in. And when someone in the choicemaker role refuses to make choices or delays making them for too long, the other energies devolve into a power struggle over which of them will take over the choicemaker's throne.

The Core Archetypes as Transformational Catalysts

You now understand the transformational nature of these five core archetypes. Each brings a critical capacity and energy that we believe is required for businesses to successfully participate in the transformational economy. We recommend that you and your executive team carefully consider the value of embracing them in the design and operation of your C-suite so you can more sustainably thrive through the chaos.

The Corporate Domains of Wisdom

Individual and group qualities of beingness, doingness, stability, change, and choicemaking show up in C-Suite roles and define the key corporate domains of business wisdom.

What archetypal role does the CEO occupy? Easy: the Choicemaker (the Sovereign). What archetypal role does the CFO occupy (in addition to legal, policy compliance, quality control, and the dominant aspects of HR)? Stability (the Steward).

Now things get more interesting. Which roles are primarily responsible for enacting transformation and change (the Magician)? R&D (that's easy), and also Marketing and Sales. Why? Because brilliant marketing and revenue generation, as well as the shadow side of unethical marketing and manipulative selling strategies, are about transforming perception by the public.

Businesses that are over-focused on transformation tend to be chaotic because the Steward's voice has been drowned out, just as businesses that are over-focused on stability tend to stifle the creativity of the Magicians.

For instance, how many battles have you seen between R&D Magicians and the CFO's insistence on Stewarding? This causes the well-known *Innovator's Dilemma*, well documented by Clayton Christensen where successful companies crash and burn when the market changes. That's an example of the counterbalance between stability and change duking it out over which is more important, when in fact both are equally important to a business's success.

What is the archetypal role the COO occupies? You probably nailed it: Doing (the Warrior).

Here's where things get the juiciest of all. Recall the counterbalancing energy of Doing is Being. What happens when Doing (Warrior) overtakes Being (Lover)? Workaholism, which of course leads to burnout. On the other hand, what happens when being nurturing and supportive Being (Lover) overtakes productivity? The business grinds to a halt.

Yet, where is the officer responsible for Beingness (Lover)?

Corporate executive structure design has ignored the role of Beingness (Lover) because of an old paradigm that people are a commodity and can be easily replaced. The result: the universal challenge of finding good people to fill key roles, lack of employee engagement, frequent job hopping, and little if any team loyalty.

The Gig Economy is the result of employees taking control of their career path in the absence of corporate support.

Let's explore what happens when you intentionally add Lover energy to an organization's leadership to counterbalance Warrior energy.

Insights from the Harvard Negotiation Project

The counterbalance between Being and Doing is what the Harvard Negotiation Project[4] inadvertently discovered when they identified the consequences of insistent hard focus or relaxed soft focus on tasks and people.

The essence of these findings:

❑ Being soft (compassionate, nurturing) on people and soft on tasks (no accountability) breeds a culture where everyone loves each other but yields low productivity.

❑ Being hard on people and soft on tasks breeds a culture where people feel ashamed or hate each other and yet produces low productivity.

❑ Being hard on people and hard on tasks breeds a temporarily productive culture where people hate each other or take advantage of each other.

❑ And being soft on people and hard on tasks breeds a high productivity, high happiness culture.
See Figure 5.

---

[4] www.pon.harvard.edu/category/research_projects/harvard-negotiation-project/

Soft on People

	Soft on People	
Soft on Tasks	Unproductive, everyone loves each other	Highly productive, high happiness
	Unproductive, everyone hates each other or feels ashamed	Temporarily productive, people hate and take advantage of each other

Soft on Tasks   **Hard on Tasks**

Hard on People

Figure 5: The Harvard Negotiation Project Observations about Hard Focus versus Soft Focus on Tasks and People

Our interpretation of this study is that under the new demands of social responsibility, a balance between Warrior (task accountability) and Lover (nurturance) becomes critical to a sustainable business.

Are you getting a feel for how archetypes synergize with or are at war against each other influences the functioning of and collaboration among your C-Suite executives and through that, the effectiveness and success of your entire business?

The Missing Archetype in C-Suites and Businesses

Holding these ideas in mind reveals the huge blind spot preventing businesses from becoming a better version of themselves so they can help their customers become better versions of themselves.

Walk through this with us:

❑ Your C-Suite includes executives whose primary domain is Stability (CFO), Change (CRO), Doing (COO),
and Choicemaking (CEO).

❑ Your C-Suite is most probability missing an executive
responsible for Being (Lover).

❑ Does the realm of Being deserve a place in your C-
Suite?

❑ If so, what is its chief officer's roles and responsibilities?

We see that the missing ingredient for a successful socially responsible, transformation business is the presence of a strategic officer responsible for bringing Lover
energy to the operation.

A radical idea? Yes, and the key idea that accelerates
TBL and ESG companies to top performance.

And no, you don't necessarily have to call them the
Chief Love Officer. We have an even more accurate title
for you.

> SOCIAL RESPONSIBILITY NOT BASED IN LOVE
> IS JUST A MANIPULATIVE EMPTY PROMISE.

The seminal work of Steve Farber on how love is
good business (in fact, one of his books is titled *Love is
Just Damn Good Business*) has been opening a lot of otherwise conventional businesses to embracing the rightful
place of love in maintaining sustained and growing prof-
itability. For that we are deeply grateful!

The Rightful Role of Corporate Love

Love takes two equally important forms: *nurturance* and
challenge. Nurturance focuses on empathy, support,

building people up, and healing wounds. Challenge focuses on growth, accountability, and stretching beyond the status quo. This is our upleveled version of Harvard's soft-on-people and hard-on-task research findings.

Nurturance without challenge is indulgence, which breeds entitlement and unproductivity. Challenge without nurturance is tyranny, which breeds anger, shame, resentment, rebellion, and turnover. Both the nurturing and challenging forms of love are utterly essential to building healthy cultures that generate sustained business success for an authentic socially responsible company.

These two forms of love are captured perfectly by the 20th century theologian, Reinhold Niebuhr who said that the purpose of religion is to "comfort the afflicted and afflict the comfortable." Any effective executive coach knows that their job is to deliver to each executive they assist an alchemical blend of just the right proportions of nurturance and challenge, and in the right moments.

Archetypal Wisdom Explains Why HR Typically Flounders

Who theoretically holds the responsibility for nurturance and challenge in a business? HR, that's who. This creates a massive problem for HR, however, and this in turn translates into massive confusion in most businesses.

Typically, HR wears two hats: *compliance* and *talent development*. Compliance is part of the Steward archetype's domain. Development is part of the Lover archetype's domain.

Blending Steward and Lover energies into a single role makes excellence in either impossible. Lack of business archetypal wisdom has allowed this blindspot to go unchecked during the decades since the inception of HR when it replaced the personnel department. And this in turn is why HR has, in many circles, been referred to as the Department of Human Remains.

Nimble businesses have an elegant solution to this dilemma: they split HR into the two separate functions they have always held – talent development (Lover) and compliance (Steward) – so each function can excel without being held back by the other.

The Need for Balanced Nurturance and Challenge

What's missing is the balance of team nurturance and team challenge, the corporate love dynamic. Dysfunction results when either of these two important motivational factors is over-energized or under-energized.

We have a society of low challenge, high nurturance resulting in rampant entitled narcissism resulting in low productivity. Your corporate culture must reject this if it is to become nimble. Here's why.

Where there is low challenge and low nurturance, there is no meaningful performance, employees do the least acceptable job, resulting in a divisive culture, low competitiveness and profits, and susceptibility to theft and corporate piracy.

High challenge and low nurturance results in a cutthroat culture where the ends justify the means, resulting in an angry, resentful team and a toxic brand experience.

High challenge and high nurturance results in an organization that functions optimally, both at the individual and team level, resulting in a stellar brand experience, and high competitiveness and profits. This is corporate Nirvana, the business version of Heaven on Earth.

See Figure 6.

High Nurturance

Indulgent, Low Productivity, Entitled	Corporate Heaven on Earth, Optimal Individual and Team Performance, Stellar Brand Reputation

Low Challenge   **High Challenge**

Low Performance, Divisive Culture, Piracy Susceptibility	Angry, Resentful, Ends Justifies the Means, Cut-Throat Culture

Low Nurturance

Figure 6: The Corporate Love Dynamic — Examining the Impact of Challenge and Nurturance on Performance

Introducing the Nimble C-Suite Organizational Structure

As mentioned before, the CEO is the Choicemaker (Sovereign), being the chief visionary, strategist, and public face of the business.

> **A CEO** WHO PASSES THE BUCK IS A FIGUREHEAD, NOT A LEADER.

They are the final choicemaker about how decisions will be made; the buck stops with them. In the role of challenge, they function like an orchestra conductor who ensures the high performance, synchronized collaboration with the other players. And in the role of nurturance, they generously reach out to bless all who have positive business impact.

In turn, the other C-Suite executives are the strategy-focused Sovereigns of their own archetypal wisdom realms who closely coordinate with each other and the CEO to ensure optimal strategic collaboration and minimal siloing.

> EACH C-SUITE EXECUTIVE IS THE SOVEREIGN OF THEIR REALM.

Just as the C-Suite executives are the CEO's key strategic advisors, they each have archetypally key tactical advisors (VPs or Directors) who report to them, just as those tactical advisors have archetypally key managers or team leaders and implementers who report to them.

By *archetypally key* we mean that each Executive, VP, Director, and Manager is surrounded by people who collectively cover all four of the outer archetypes – Being, Doing, Stability, and Change – in their realm.

Built In Succession Planning

The implementation of archetypally key teams under each department head means that team members with key skills naturally understand how to collaborate as an aligned team.

You can identify those who align with specific archetypes because they will naturally and enthusiastically bring excellence to their role. This solves the motivational issues that plague most companies. With programmatic mindset and skills development directed by the executive with the Lover archetype, you'll be able to promote leaders from within who are willing, ready-skilled, and culturally aligned.

This means that you don't have to do developmental executive rotations through roles that they aren't well suited for, which is a well-meaning, but unnecessary cause of corporate dysfunction and upheaval. In a later chapter on temperament, we'll unpack why this common practice cannot yield predictable results.

This substantially reduces stress and underperformance, as each team member always operates from their zone of genius. Let the Stewards be stewards, the Warriors be warriors, and Sovereigns be sovereigns. Don't make a Warrior be a Lover or a Steward be a Magician; they don't like it and it kills corporate performance.

Archetypal competence imbues your organization with *Succession Competence*, where every team lead understands how to promote and be promoted. This is what we mean by aligning the diverse skills of your team for predictable results.

The Five Functions of the Nimble C-Suite

Before we explore what this looks like, we want to acknowledge that we are about to disrupt the fundamental structure of the C-Suite because when it realigns around the Core Archetypes, it ends up streamlining into only four strategically-focused executives plus the CEO.

We call the executive overseeing the company's Stability (Steward) functions the *Sustainability Officer*. Not the version of sustainability that has to do with environmental considerations – that falls under another archetype we'll get to shortly – but rather the financial sustainability of the business itself.

We call the executive overseeing the company's Transformation (Magician) functions the *Revenue Officer*.

We call the executive overseeing the company's Doingness (Warrior) functions the *Operations Officer*.

And we call the executive overseeing the company's Beingness (Lover) functions the *Integrity Officer*.

See Figure 7.

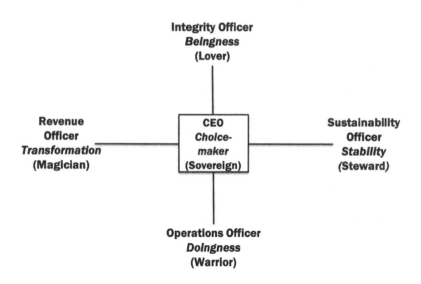

Figure 7: Corporate Officers Aligned with the Necessary Actions and Archetypes of a Nimble Organization

Let's take a closer look at each of these roles reporting to the Choicemaker (Sovereign) Chief Executive Officer.

The Sustainability Officer (Steward Archetype)

The Sustainability Officer is responsible for strategizing and overseeing business functions primarily related to stability, predictability, organization, and standards.

The domain of the Sustainability Officer includes financial stewardship, legal stewardship, securing data assets and physical assets, compliance, and evaluation standards.

The VP or Director responsibilities that belong under the Sustainability Officer include cash flow management, accounting, credit, debt, legal compliance, data policy and compliance, security and risk mitigation, quality control, compliance with guiding principles and policies, and ensuring that what is taught in protocol training programs is consistently used.

The Revenue Officer (Magician Archetype)

The Revenue Officer is responsible for strategizing and overseeing business functions primarily related to foreseeing future trends, creative and proactive preparation for capturing new mission-aligned market opportunities, and manifesting revenue in the now, the near term, and the long term.

The domain of the Revenue Officer includes business development (marketing and sales) and R&D.

Examples of VP or Director responsibilities that belong under the Revenue Officer include new product development, marketing, and sales, and accounts receivable (because accrual accounting practices aside, it's not revenue until you're paid).

The Operations Officer (Warrior Archetype)

The Operations Officer is responsible for strategizing and overseeing business functions primarily related to persistent, effortful, forward movement in producing and providing what the company sells.

The domain of the Operations Officer includes ensuring that what's sold is built and delivered with superb quality and that the customer experience is equally superb.

Examples of VP or Director responsibilities that belong under the Operations Officer include supply chain management, the data processing center, vendor relations, manufacturing, logistics and delivery, customer service, and customer satisfaction.

The Integrity Officer (Lover Archetype)

The Integrity Officer is responsible for strategizing and overseeing business functions primarily related to ensuring that the business is operating in alignment with the Triple Bottom Line (TBL) of a socially responsible ESG business.

The domain of the Integrity Officer includes overseeing personnel and culture development and ensuring brand integrity perception through TBL/ESG alignment and environmental sustainability. Done right, this brings unbeatable non-product-based brand differentiation that competitors can't easily duplicate. The Integrity Officer is the CEO's secret weapon to market domination in a transformational economy.

Examples of VP or Director responsibilities that belong under the Integrity Officer include skills training, personnel engagement and development, culture installation, customer experience design, environmental responsibility, public relations, and reputation management.

Why This Alignment is Essential to Your Success

Strategy and tactics are equally important. However, strategy requires a different lens from tactics, which illuminates the sequencing necessary for wise tactics selection. Properly sequenced tactics implementation makes it possible to nimbly, efficiently, and profitably achieve the mission goals that bring your vision to reality.

> DON'T ASK A STRATEGIST TO MAKE TACTICAL DECISIONS OR IMPLEMENT THEM, DON'T ASK A TACTICIAN TO STRATEGIZE, AND DON'T ASK AN IMPLEMENTER TO SEQUENCE.

Sorting executive roles into strategic and tactical eliminate unnecessary C-Suite conflict and gridlock caused by the vast lens differences between strategists and tactics selectors. Can you see the leadership advantage this brings you?

The lens differences, necessarily built into each role for overall checks and balances, make it challenging enough for strategists to collaborate with strategists and for tacticians to collaborate with tacticians. Simultaneously dealing with strategic and tactical lens differences becomes unmanageably inefficient. The conflicts that arise from trying to do this create unnecessary, avoidable upheavals.

It's far more efficient for strategic executives of the strategic S-Suite to pool their vast lens differences to develop a strategy that they can then bring to tactical T-

Suite executives for their perspective, often around timing.

Then, once final strategic decisions are made based on that input, the S-Suite's job is to hand off these to the T-Suite so those tactically focused executives can make decisions about sequenced implementation and then can identify required resources.

Challenges Implementing This Structure

Your head may be swimming with questions and concerns about how to deploy this in your company. Stay with us. We're not done yet.

Dividing your C-Suite into an S-Suite and a T-Suite will trigger fear. However, this is a healthy and necessary kind of upheaval for companies to undergo that are pivoting to the TBL/ESG model and the Transformation Economy. We don't know how you can otherwise get there without much pain, suffering and ultimately the risk of going out of business.

Executives who don't know how to manage their fear while exploring new approaches to their roles and responsibilities do not have sufficient psychological savvy to function as nimble executives. This is a red flag.

In contrast, executives who do have this psychological savvy recognize that leading edge leaders require leading edge upleveling. Because of this, they will be exhilarated by the process of discovering how to reassign responsibilities for maximal leverage so they align with the diverse strengths of each archetypally-based S-Suite or T-Suite position. Plus, they get to operate far more effortlessly and joyously within their personal zone of genius. This becomes your well-oiled machine.

As we write the first edition of this book, few examples exist of archetypally realigned S-Suites and T-Suites. However, we have successfully deployed this kind of approach with clients and have even acted as interim Integrity Officers for some.

Your Payoff for This Work

A Nimble C-Suite comprised of an S-Suite and T-Suite provides potential business buyers with a highly reliable operating system that they will find compellingly attractive. This is because investors today have four motivations to buy: operations, business potential, cash flow, and TBL alignment. Businesses that fruitfully operate in all of these areas fetch the highest price.

Therefore, those who own a business that they eventually want to sell would be well-advised to develop it in archetypally aligned ways, to split their C-Suite into an S-Suite and T-Suite, and to add an Integrity Officer to their S-Suite.

Chapter Summary

❑ There are three ways to form and organize your C-Suite: 1) Inherited, 2) Inertia, and 3) Designed. Given today's chronic upheavals and the unstoppable movement toward corporate social responsibility with TBL and ESG, only the Designed option can work.

❑ The five core archetypes with their respective domains of wisdom essential for today's effective business are Stability (Steward), Doingness (Warrior), Transformation (Magician), Beingness (Lover), and Choicemaking (Sovereign).

- ❑ Five core archetypes point the way to C-Suite Nimbility and to separating the C-Suite into a strategic S-Suite and a tactical T-Suite.
- ❑ An archetypally aligned C-Suite (S-Suite plus T-Suite) and resulting archetypally aligned company structure provides the most streamlined and reliable way to ensure psychological diversity and minimize blind spots.
- ❑ The S-Suite is exclusively comprised of strategists, each of whom provide the primary strategic wisdom of each of the core archetypes.
- ❑ Each S-Suite executive has Vice Presidents or Directors who provide primary tactical wisdom for each core archetype in that executive's strategic realm.
- ❑ Vice Presidents (if needed) interface between strategic and tactical functions, Directors orchestrate tactical implementation, and Team Leaders manage their team's implementation.
- ❑ Succession Competence is built into this archetypally based structure. You'll always have promotable talent ready, willing, and able.
- ❑ Shadow expressions of the archetypes result in difficult employees and dysfunctional company cultures. You eliminate these through accountability overseen by the Choicemaker and Lover functions.
- ❑ Business archetypal alignment virtually eliminates blind spots, piracy, and other factors that make businesses unnecessarily susceptible to avoidable upheavals.

Ask Yourself

☐ Does this archetypally aligned way of reorganizing my C-Suite into an S-Suite and T-Suite address the challenges I'm facing today?

☐ Can I continue down the path I'm on right now, or do I need to make radical changes, knowing that radical becomes acceptable becomes normal becomes historic?

☐ Does this make sense, even if it's a radical approach?

☐ Does this allow me to differentiate and stand out from my competition in a non-product way?

☐ Which of the five core archetypes are currently under-represented in my C-Suite?

☐ Which of my current C-Suite roles are actually tactical, Vice President roles?

☐ Which of my current C-Suite roles are actually tactical, Director roles?

☐ Which of my current C-Suite executives are struggling to fulfill their role because they are wearing two or more archetypal hats?

☐ If I transition to a nimble C-Suite structure, what problems might that resolve and what opportunities might that open?

☐ If I choose to not make the transition, what might be the cost, short and long term?

☐ How might I organize my S-Suite and T-Suite?

Ask Your Team

☐ What do you see as the barriers to us becoming an authentic socially responsible company?

{ 81 }

❑ What frustrations and inefficiencies do you experience because you're required to constantly switch between strategic and tactical roles?

❑ Do you see a clear path for promotion and career advancement for your team and yourself?

❑ Do you feel that your natural abilities are recognized and well used? If not, what might be a role that is better aligned with your true talent?

Action Plan

❑ Internalize the framework in this chapter by contemplating your answers to the "Ask Yourself" questions above. If you would benefit from discussing these questions, engage the NimbilityWorks™ team to catalyze your clarity. Learn more on page 219.

❑ Have your team leaders answer the "Ask Your Team" questions above.

❑ Use your best judgment on how to proceed based on your research with these questions.

❑ Train your executive team in this chapter's framework or bring in a NimbilityWorks partner to provide this training.

❑ Develop a plan for upleveling your organizational structure based on what emerges from the above Action Plan steps. Use our help. Consult with the NimbilityWorks team as useful. See more on page 219.

Chapter 4:
Key Elements of Nimble Executive Temperament

Now that you understand the required archetypal structure, let's look at the required executive temperament for success in each role.

A psychologically savvy executive intentionally takes temperament factors into account when placing team members in roles. A mismatch limits Nimbility, causes underperformance, stifles collaboration, and triggers upheavals. A match enables Nimbility, accelerates collaboration, and eliminates much stress, as the team member's temperament is aligned with their role, so they operate naturally in their zone of genius.

The Impact of Temperament on Role Performance

Each executive role must look at business opportunities, challenges, and decisions through a very different lens from other executives. Appreciating this can create a strong executive team. Not appreciating this creates yet another source of avoidable upheavals.

For this reason, we believe that you'll benefit from understanding necessary differences in executive *temperament*. In this chapter we'll look at the kind of temperament each executive role requires, and how each executive's temperamental lens profoundly influences their perspectives, choices, behavior, and performance.

Everyone's world view has been formed by their personal identity, culture, their personal experiences, roles and responsibilities, and the extent of their personal growth, including the quality and quantity of mentoring and coaching they have received.

Understanding the different varieties of executive temperaments can guide you in making changes with minimal disruption and can enlighten you on why you face certain challenges and obstacles and how to best approach solving them.

> LEADERS LEAD AT THE LEVEL OF THEIR SELF-DEVELOPMENT
> BLIND SPOTS DESPITE THEIR HIGHEST INTENTIONS.
> – DAVID GRUDER

First, we'll look at the components of the business ecosystem that is required to operate a sustainable, scalable operation, and the thought processes required for each element.

Second, we'll examine the critical temperament components required for controlling each component.

In the next chapter, we'll examine the critical temperament components required for each executive role.

Systems View versus Procedures View

Each executive role takes on a domain within the business ecosystem, with higher-level roles being responsible for a broader, longer-term viewpoint and lower-level roles being responsible for a narrower slice with a shorter timeframe. This structure allows us to break up the business into smaller chunks and associate them with specific planning processes and assignments of roles and responsibilities. It allows you to see the business components in context. We also use it as a map to troubleshoot systems problems.

Let's first look at the business ecosystem as a series of nested functions. See Figure 8.

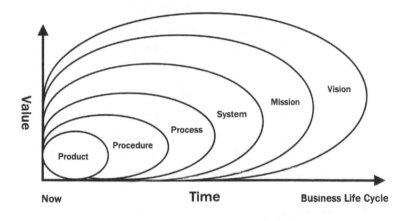

Figure 8: Business Ecosystem Components — Nesting Functions with Increasing Cumulative Value and Timespans

The horizontal axis represents *time,* from this moment to the end of the business lifecycle (closure or acquisition), and the vertical axis represents the relative *value* of the function to the corporation. For example, a specific product changes most rapidly, so has the shortest timeline and the least cumulative value. Vision and mission have the longest time range because they don't change very rapidly and therefore have more cumulative value.

Complexity increases as we move toward the right of the timeline, requiring increased cognitive capacity to manage that complexity. In addition, the further in the future that one must plan, the more cognitive capacity is required, as long-term planning requires dealing with increasing uncertainty. This is why top officers must have high cognitive capacity to operate effectively.

> AN EFFECTIVE EXECUTIVE MUST POSSESS
> THE COGNITIVE CAPACITY TO HANDLE THE COMPLEXITY
> OF THE PART OF THE ORGANIZATION THEY DIRECT.

The *Vision* has the greatest cumulative value and longest-term impact on the organization and describes what will be manifested. A company's vision is the difference they want to make in the world, the corporate legacy, as a result of profitably providing their products or services.

For corporations, their mission is to make money. For governments, their mission is to protect and advance the wellbeing of the population. For education, its mission is to produce highly functioning graduates who generate a strong return on their time and tuition investment.

The *Mission*, that part of the vision which is actively being manifested, determines the types of products, services, and experiences that can best accomplish it.

Systems are the building blocks that make up the business model: product, marketing, sales, finance, etc. This is the architecture of the business. We discuss the common system elements in detail in the companion to this book, *The Nimble Company*.

Processes compose the system building blocks, such as the sales process, marketing process, financial processes, etc. Processes are almost always designed and controlled in-house.

Procedures define the details of the business model implementation and the tactical actions that, when combined, form the processes. This includes initiatives, such as developing a new product, launching a new product, marketing campaigns, sales demonstrations, cash flow modeling, etc. Procedures will change as vendors change, technology changes, and the labor pool changes. A procedure may be outsourced or performed in-house.

The *Product* is the outcome of the procedures, whether a good or service. Producing new products will use many of the established procedures and yet will likely require modification, elimination, or introduction of new procedures.

Each of these ecosystem elements require a different thought process to architect and implement. See Figure 9.

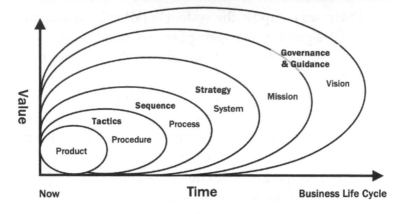

Figure 9: Business Ecosystem — Interaction of System Actions (Strategy, Tactics, etc.) on the Ecosystem Elements

Mission and vision require *governance and guidance*. Systems design requires *strategy*, which sets the blueprint for the organization's operations. Processes demand *sequencing*, the order in which actions are accomplished. Procedures are the specific *tactics* that produce the product, ensure an accountable culture, and provide superb customer experiences with the product and company.

Responsibility for each of these components determines team design and who reports to whom about what. While it's possible for one person to perform multiple roles, often the case in smaller organizations, the complexity of most companies demands that one person becomes responsible for oversight of each element. See Figure 10.

{ 88 }

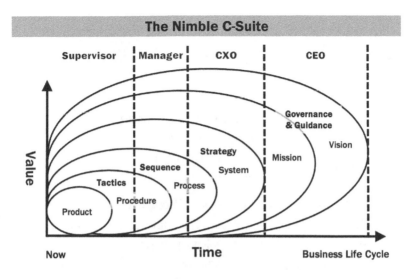

Figure 10: Business Ecosystem — Roles and Responsibilities
for Each of the Key Ecosystem Elements

Leadership requirements are different for each of the ecosystem elements. The *Board of Directors* and *CEO* are responsible governance and guidance, acting as the architects for the business and defining the necessary system. The *CXOs*, those chiefs responsible for overseeing the business execution building blocks, orchestrate the processes. *Managers* determine sequencing of the procedures. *Supervisors* determine the implementation of the procedures performed by the implementors.

Use this model to identify misalignment of roles and responsibilities because this causes and fosters upheavals.

KPIs Drive Executive Decisions

An executive's world view is driven by their vision, mission, and selected key results as measured by their key performance indicator (KPI). If you use OKRs (Objectives

{ 89 }

and Key Results) just substitute OKR for KPI as you read this.

> **KPIs ARE HOW EXECUTIVES KEEP THEIR JOB.**
> **WHEN IT'S OKAY, THEY STAY.**
> **WHEN IT'S LOW, THEY GO.**

In general, if an action doesn't contribute to improving the KPI it is connected to, that action gets assigned to someone else, or it becomes low priority.

This means that if you ask an executive to perform a task that doesn't support their KPIs, they'll refuse, or ignore it. And rightly so; distraction from their KPIs brings well-documented career risk.

We discuss in depth how to select meaningful, nimble KPIs in the companion book, *The Nimble Company*.

Just as correct KPIs are set by objectives and strategy, each executive's success in meeting those is set by the extent to which their temperament aligns with their role.

For example, a CEO is usually measured by profit and growth, often benchmarked against their industry and where they are in the business lifecycle (e.g., startup or mature operation).

Strategy is a big picture activity, looking at the entire organization and associated systems. It's not a detailed look but instead seeing all the parts as a whole. We call seeing the big picture *topsight*, or the 30,000-foot view.

The Ability to Foresee the Future

An important part of strategy is how an executive looks forward in time, their *foresight*. Each executive becomes responsible for a different time horizon, depending on how strategic or how tactical their role demands.

Here are the five time horizons we use to evaluate required foresight:[5]

❑ 0-6 months – Market Chasing: Looking for ways to optimize sales by pursuing markets who buy right now. Usually the role of sales.

❑ 6-18 months – Need Seeking: Identifying the new needs of the customer to adapt current offerings to their changing desires and requirements. Usually the role of marketing.

❑ 18-36 months – Tech Innovating: Inventing new technology and innovating with current technology to retain current customers and capture future customers. Usually the role of R&D, often in conjunction with operations.

❑ 36-72 months – Culture Tracking: Identifying culture shifts that impact future customer decisions. Usually the role of top executives.

❑ 72+ months – Legacy Planning: Considering how the company vision can be directed for long term success. Usually the role of the CEO and Board of Directors.

The Aspects of Resources Outlook Impact Prioritization

Sequencing of objectives determines the priorities, and the order in which they are focused to get the mission accomplished. Priorities set an executive's relationship with

---

[5] A tip of the hat to Magnus Pinker for defining the first three horizons.

key corporate resources. Let's look at resource relationships that impact priorities and as such, impact sequencing choices.

- ❑ View of Data: Do they curate, create, or consume data? We explore this in detail in the companion book, *The Nimble Company*.
- ❑ View of Money: Do they set budgets, audit budgets, or spend budgets?
- ❑ View of Team: Are they systems aware or team aware?
- ❑ View of Assets: Do they plan assets, deploy assets, or use assets?
- ❑ View of Resilience and Risk: Do they accept risk, are aware of risk, or avoid risk? High resilience results in lower risk because of the ability to rapidly recover from an undesired state.
- ❑ Level of Nimbility: Are they stuck, open, or nimble?

Do you see how a person relates to each of these dimensions impacts how they will naturally make priority and sequencing decisions? This must influence your choice of role for the person.

For example, you don't want a risk accepting CFO (you want risk aware) nor do you want a risk averse CRO or they'd never talk with new customers.

The Impact Adrenaline Tolerance on Perceived Risk

View of risk is partially determined by one's physical response to adrenaline, the fight-or-flight hormone triggered by perceived risk. If you like the feeling of adrenaline – heart racing, mind sharpening, muscles tensing – you'll seek activities that trigger adrenaline release, often perceived as *risk seeking*. If you don't like that feeling, you'll be *risk averse*.

You may have observed that some top executives crave adrenaline-triggering activities that others perceive as high risk. For example:

- ❑ Oracle CEO, Larry Ellison, captains the world's fastest sailboats and engages in acrobatic airplane racing
- ❑ Virgin CEO, Richard Branson, pilots a hot air balloon a record-breaking 6,700 miles
- ❑ Amazon founder, Jeff Bezos, rockets into space
- ❑ Google exec, Alan Eustace, skydives from a balloon at a world-record 136,000 feet.

As a leader, you're more likely to enjoy exciting activities, like racing cars, riding motorcycles, and enjoying rollercoasters. Your risk averse team, such as the CIO, probably more enjoys less risky activities, like playing golf, fishing, or watching sports. When planning team activities, poll them to see what brings them pleasure instead of falling into the trap of thinking that what makes you excited is what makes them excited. It's not about courage, but about how each person physically reacts to different adrenaline levels.

Criteria Drives Decisions and Tactics Selection

Criteria determine how one makes a tactical decision. Along with the view of resources listed above, criteria drive tactical choices. The three key criteria most used:

- ❑ Know: What they must they *know* to perform
- ❑ Do: What they need to physically *do* to perform
- ❑ Feel: What they desire to *feel* to perform.

How Feelings Drive Decisions

You've heard that people make decisions based on emotion and then justify those choices with logic. While this may appear to be illogical, it's true. The desired feeling is that *gut check* response of decision making.

> EMOTION IS THE PHYSICAL SENSATION
> WE ARE PAYING ATTENTION TO AND LABELING RIGHT NOW.
> – TONY BODOH

Feelings are physical sensations driven by hormones and brain chemistry, triggered by environmental factors or thought patterns. We tend to label these sensations, with those labels determining how we interpret our feelings. What one person might label as fear another might label as excitement, even though both are triggered by identical brain chemistry.

The desired feeling drives the physiological interpretation. For those with lower adrenaline tolerance, this means feeling risk-free. For those with higher adrenaline tolerance, this means feeling excited.

For example, a CEO makes decisions based on feeling *confident* (expecting a positive outcome), a CFO makes decisions based on feeling *comfortable* (expecting that risks will be well-managed), a COO makes decisions based on feeling *certain* (expecting that systems will remain under control and function at peak efficiency).

> FEAR IS THE EXPECTATION OF AN UNDESIRABLE OUTCOME.
> CONFIDENCE IS THE EXPECTATION OF A DESIRABLE OUTCOME.

Perspective Drives Communication Style

One's worldview gets expressed through how they communicate their thoughts. Communication style tends to be based on temperament and is impacted by that person's attitude about each current, high priority task. Each aspect of communication falls on a spectrum, ranging from one approach to an opposite counterbalancing approach. Rather than judging a communication style as good or bad, one's choices are about what is more resourceful for a specific task, leading to better outcomes.

Let's examine six of these dimensions. More have been defined, yet these are sufficient for our discussion.[6]

We've laid them out so that you can explore them in a two-page spread.

---

[6] For an excellent, in-depth discussion, see Shelle Rose Charvet's book *Words That Change Minds: Mastering the Language of Influence*.

Need for Information and Detail

The first dimension is one's need for information and detail, *General* versus *Specific*. A General style looks at the big picture and a Specific style focuses on the details.

A General talks in broad terms, using words such as often, always, never, sometimes. They use their imagination to fill in the blanks to see the big picture. When a General asks, "How does this work" the best answer is, "It works great!" Example roles of Generals: military generals, CEOs, and professional salespeople.

A Specific talks in detailed terms, quoting exact numbers and precise data. They require specific details to make decisions, doing research to fill in the blanks. When a Specific asks, "How does this work?" they want to see the blueprint. Examples of Specifics: engineers, IT professionals, and financial analysts.

The blind spot of a General is not seeing the trees for the forest, whereas the blind spot for a Specific is not seeing the forest for the trees. Every organization needs team members with both skills: the General to define the map and destination, and Specifics to take the journey.

> GIVE A GENERAL TOO MUCH DETAIL AND THEY DISCONNECT.
> GIVE A SPECIFIC INSUFFICIENT DETAILS AND THEY'LL BE FRUSTRATED.

Sixty percent of the population defaults to General style, 25 percent is a blend, and 15 percent defaults to Specific style. See the following chart to compare and contrast ways to communicate, persuade, motivate, and present to mixed communication styles.

General...**Specific**

60%	25%	15%
Communicate:	Be direct, bottom line, concepts No details unless they ask Use sweeping body language	Thorough, complete, precise Qualifiers Use pointed body language
Persuade:	Summarize everything Charts & graphs "The point is…"	Break into incremental steps Sequences Details
Motivate:	Align with long-term plans "How do you see this fitting into your big picture?"	Include supporting materials "What specifically do you need to be confident?"
Presenting to both:	Bullets, stories Rules of thumb Executive overview CEO proposal section	How to Lots of detail In-depth analysis CFO proposal section

Information Sorting

Information sorting describes how one compares current data to past experiences: do they look for similarities – *Match,* or differences – *Mismatch.*

Matchers find common ground, talk about shared insights ("Let's talk about what we have in common!"), agree to disagree, and like to be liked. They excel at creating community and personal relationships based on common interests yet may not be able to constructively handle conflict because they can feel that disagreement is personal. Examples of Matchers: sales professionals, marketing professionals (unless in editing mode), and leaders when focused on community-building or consensus-building.

Mismatchers identify what's out of place, talk about differences ("Why should we talk about things we agree about?"), and debate until they understand the situation. They excel at troubleshooting and keeping order, yet may not relate well to others when using their superpower in social situations in which dissimilar opinions are bandied about. Examples of Mismatchers: engineers, IT professionals, law enforcement, financial analysts.

> **EXPECT TO DEBATE WITH MISMATCHERS.**
> **EXPECT TO DISCUSS COMMON GROUND WITH MATCHERS.**

Every organization needs both styles to function correctly. Eighty percent of the population tend to Match and 20 percent tend to Mismatch. See the following chart to compare and contrast how to communicate, persuade, motivate, and present to mixed communication styles.

Match 80%	....	Mismatch 20%
Communicate:	Establish common ground "What do you like best?" Use familiar body language	Debate the issues "What are your concerns?" Use authoritative body language
Persuade:	Illustrate consensus More positives then negatives	Validate with authoritative evidence Discuss non-fatal flaws
Motivate:	Invite them along "You'll love this."	Preponderance of proof "Low probability of failure"
Presenting to both:	Social proof Popularity "Just like you..."	Suspend judgement "This is a well thought out solution." "Now you might be thinking..."

Organization and Implementation of Tasks

One's style of organizing and implementing tasks determines how they approach their role and responsibility. *Options*-oriented people see, and often use, diverse ways to complete their tasks. *Procedures*-oriented people choose the single process they deem as most effective.

Those with an Options orientation don't mind interruptions and can handle disruptions to their plans. They find excitement in change, delight in seeking alternative ways to accomplish an outcome, and get frustrated when they see a better path that they don't feel free to take. Examples of Options-oriented roles: sales professionals, leadership, inventors.

Procedures-oriented people execute to their defined process and dislike interruptions or changes to their procedure. They find comfort in taking known steps and get frustrated when asked to make changes, because that brings risk of failure, something to be avoided. Examples of Procedures-oriented roles: IT professionals, legal, accounting.

YOU MUST SCHEDULE TIME WITH PROCEDURES.
YOU CAN DROP IN ON OPTIONS.

Every company needs a blend of these two styles to be sustainable. Forty percent of the population tend to be Options-oriented, 40 percent tend to be Procedures-oriented, and 20 percent have a flexible style that blends both. See the following chart to compare and contrast how to communicate, persuade, motivate, and present to mixed communication styles.

Options .... **Procedures**

40%	20%	40%
Communicate:	Be flexible, let them jump around Possibility Choices and changes Use varied body motions	Stay on track Probability Numerated sequence Use ordered body motions
Persuade:	The best of the available choices based on their criteria Change the rules	Lead to single, logical choice Proven methodology By the rules
Motivate:	Offer a set of alternatives Revolutionary Deadlines	Structured decision making Evolutionary Next step
Presenting to both:	Headlines Bullets Questions Table of Contents	Story Logical progression Enumeration Worksheets

Locus of Motivation

This spectrum examines the source (or locus) of one's motivation, determined by how they judge if they're doing well or not. Everyone wants to do well, yet how they determine this varies by their style. *Internals* use their moral compass to judge their personal actions. *Externals* use outside feedback to determine if they are on track.

Internals know they've performed well when they feel they've done their best. They aren't strongly influenced by external factors, such as others' opinions, or mass popularity. They laugh at gamification. Since they are motivated by their own volition, they can work on long-term projects without seeing much external proof of success. They tend to do well creating strategy and don't require external feedback to stay on track. If you want to reward them, send a donation to their favorite charity in their name. Examples of Internals: strategic leaders, inventors, and professional helpers such as therapists.

Externals know they've performed well when others have told them so. They seek accolades, awards, and public recognition. They love gamification. They are influenced by popularity and status. For this reason, they work best on short-term projects with instant feedback because they need a constant stream of reinforcement to stay on track. They tend to do well executing tactics. Examples of Externals: sales professionals (specifically those who will work tirelessly for a $50 plaque and peer recognition), marketing professionals, tactical implementers.

> USING EXTERNAL MOTIVATION METHODS FAIL
> FOR INTERNALLY MOTIVATED PEOPLE. AND VICE VERSA.

Both styles are required in different roles to be sustainable and scalable. Forty percent of the population tend to be Internals, 40 percent tend to be Externals, and 20 percent have a flexible style that blends both.

Internal.. External		
40%	**20%**	**40%**
Communicate:	Ask questions "How will you know what to choose?" Point to self	Offer opinions, testimonials Recommendations Point to others
Persuade:	Suggest based on their experiences What factors have you used in the past to decide – it's just like that	Appeal to what others think Awards, best in class
Motivate:	Align with their personal vision What do you think? Make sure you consider…	Endorsements by those they respect You'll look good You'll make quite an impact
Presenting to both:	Your success stories What's in it for them How to justify it for themselves	Other's success stories What's in it for others How to justify it to others

Level of Initiative

Level of initiative defines how one approaches new projects: *Proactives* actively initiate and *Reactives* respond to initiation by others.

Proactives don't wait for others direction to get started. They make things happen. They are really good at innovating and starting projects. They tend to have many projects open and may not be good at bringing them to completion. Examples of Proactives: CEOs, inventors, entrepreneurs, sales professionals.

Reactives respond to directions, following orders. They are good at executing procedures. They like to work at one task at a time and to follow them to completion. Don't ask them to multitask, it confuses them. Asking them to innovate activates stress rather than delight. Examples of Reactives: front line employees, finance personnel, technical support staff.

DON'T EXPECT REACTIVES TO INNOVATE.

Your organization needs both to succeed, as Proactives need to set the goals and Reactives need to follow the orders that make it possible to hit those goals. Twenty percent of the population tend to be Proactives, 20 percent tend to be Reactives, and 60 percent have a flexible style that blends both. See the following chart to compare and contrast how to communicate, persuade, motivate, and present to mixed communication styles.

Proactive .... Reactive		
20%	**60%**	**20%**
Communicate:	Everything is their idea Urgency Action words Energetic body language	Advise, spell it out Clarification Consideration and consensus Reserved body language
Persuade:	Something to say "yes" to "When will you make this happen?"	Prescribe specific solutions "When is this likely to happen?"
Motivate:	Initiate, expedite everything Tie to their priorities Use Urgency	Push gently, involve others Tie to other's priorities Use Deadlines
Presenting to both:	Interactive discussions Ask questions to sell themselves "How will you know when it's time to commit?"	Be entertaining "What do I need to clarify?" "What must happen for your team to proceed?"

View of Objectives

The last spectrum to consider is one's view of objectives: do they drive *Toward* a goal or move *Away* from an undesired outcome.

Toward-types desire to achieve an objective, gain an outcome, accomplish a target. They tend to be optimistic, enthusiastic, and confident. They tend to underestimate the obstacles and limits and overestimate the opportunities and environment. Examples of Toward-types: CEOs, sales professionals.

Away-types attempt to limit risk, avoid an undesired outcome, and stay out of trouble. They tend to be pessimistic, reserved, and uncertain. They tend to overestimate the barriers and challenges and underestimate the paybacks and rewards. Examples of Away-types: legal, financial, compliance.

> AWAY-TYPES FIND LONG-RANGE PLANNING STRESSFUL BECAUSE THE IMAGINED OBSTACLES OVERWHELM THEM.

Both styles are required in different roles to be sustainable and scalable. Forty percent of the population tend to be Towards, 40 percent tend to be Aways, and 20 percent have a flexible style that blends both. See the following chart to compare and contrast how to communicate, persuade, motivate, and present to mixed communication styles.

Toward.. Away		
40%	**20%**	**40%**
Communicate:	Potential positive outcomes to gain Use inclusive body language	Potential negative outcomes to avoid Use excluding body language
Persuade:	Return on investment Value of the potential gains	Opportunity cost Impact of the potential losses
Motivate:	Seeking pleasure Recognition of a bold choice	Avoiding pain Recognition of a prudent choice
Presenting to both:	The worth of moving forward Discuss dreams come true	The cost of things remaining as they are Discuss pain avoided

Using Communication Styles to Your Benefit

The tension among the styles creates the dynamic of forward momentum and stability required in a nimble organization. If one style becomes over-energized, upheavals tend to result.

If one is in a role that requires a General-Proactive-Toward style, such as a CEO, if their natural tendency is to exhibit Specific-Reactive-Away styles, this is a styles misalignment that gridlocks their effectiveness and creates a stuck organization. Or conversely, a role where a Specific-Reactive-Away style is required, such as a CIO, when the leader occupying this role doesn't have this style blend, instability is often the result.

We've found that much conflict in an organization comes from team members not understanding, or even disrespecting, the styles that are required for each role and responsibility. Fix this with role-style alignment, communications styles training, and troubleshooting tactics.[7]

A NIMBLE CEO KNOWS THAT TO HAVE MAXIMUM IMPACT,
THEY MUST USE THE COMMUNICATION STYLE THAT IS
LEAST STRESSFUL TO THE ONE THEY'RE COMMUNICATING WITH.

If you're challenged communicating with a team member, identify your style and their style. You'll immediately notice that you are on opposite ends of one or more of these spectrums. Recognizing their style and adapting your communication to that style can rapidly restore understanding and yield useful solutions.

---

[7] We can help or make recommendations.

Chapter Summary

❑ Everyone has a world view shaped by their identity, culture, training, experience, and mindset that comprises their temperament.

❑ Understanding these elements substantially increases your psychological savvy.

❑ Certain temperaments align well with certain roles and responsibilities. A psychologically savvy executive intentionally takes this into account when structuring their executive suite.

❑ A key temperament element is whether one takes a strategic, systems view or a tactical, procedures view. This can be influenced by training to understand the business ecosystem elements.

❑ The impact of cognitive capacity, the ability handle complexity, influences how one perceives the future because considering the unknown increases perceived complexity.

❑ How a person views resources such as data, money, team, assets, resilience and risk, and time determines how they prioritize tasks and influences their capacity to make decisions and execute tasks.

❑ A person's sensitivity to adrenaline has impact on how they view risk, from risk averse to risk seeking.

❑ A person's relationship with emotions determines what is an acceptable emotional state and varies widely, which impacts temperament and therefore suitability for certain roles.

❑ How one communicates impacts how they process information, approach tasks, measure success, and view risk. Each executive role needs a different communication lens for success.

❑ You and your team's understanding of the necessarily different lenses enables collaboration and respect for differing perspectives. It also greatly enhances your ability to bridge the perspective gap between the members of your executive team.

Ask Yourself

❑ How might understanding the wide-ranging perspectives of your team help better harness their diversity for more Nimbility and greater success?

❑ How might you expand your perspective to include this new understanding to better appreciate a team member who challenges you?

❑ Where do you observe friction in leading certain team members that can be explained by your new understanding of temperament?

❑ How can you expand your understanding to gain insights and enhanced collaboration?

❑ How might teaching your executive team about temperament and its impact on perspective and decision making, reduce friction and enhance collaboration through a new appreciation of each of the team member's perspectives and a new way of tapping into each other's strengths?

Ask Your Team

❑ Where do you see team member perspective clashes interfering with our ability to nimbly navigate challenging problems and limiting decision speed?

❑ Honestly, do you work with colleagues who always seem to rub you the wrong way, or they just can't seem to see or appreciate your perspective?

❑ What might happen if you saw them in a new way that might help you appreciate and harness their diversity?

❑ How effective are we as an executive team in collaborating and communicating? Where do we have gaps and opportunities?

Action Plan

❑ Get familiar with the multiple aspects and dimensions of what makes up temperament. The better you understand these dimensions, the better you can navigate conflict and communication crises.

❑ Have ongoing executive and management training about these elements to uplevel the psychological savvy of your team.

❑ When in a conflict, use the insights from this chapter to troubleshoot the cause, often a misalignment of your temperaments or your misunderstanding of their temperament.

Chapter 5:
The Nimble Executive
Temperament by Role

Now that you understand the key elements of temperament, let's examine the temperament of each of your team members. Each executive's role requires a specific temperament for success. Where there are temperament mismatches, gaps, or over-energized, or under-energized areas, problems arise, collaboration gets stifled, and role success diminishes.

The temperament analysis in the rest of this chapter describes what we see in a well-functioning organization aligned with the Nimble C-Suite design. While these are generalizations, in our experience they tend to be accurate for the vast majority of organizations.

We'll start by examining the strategic roles and then we'll review the tactical roles.

Board of Directors Temperament

While the board itself doesn't have a defined temperament, they do have a critical governance role of providing sage wisdom and guidance to the CEO and executive team. When functioning well, they are a strategic sounding board that also holds the chief executives accountable for their actions and results.

The board's noble purpose is to guide a company to manifest its corporate vision. Its deepest concern has traditionally centered around fulfilling shareholder expectations, although this is now shifting toward fulfilling the expectations of all stakeholders in alignment with TBL/ESG commitments. Its highest intention is to unleash the company leadership's potential. Motivators for board members tend to be about leaving a legacy of making a difference.

It is important for board members to understand how executive temperaments interact, and how these interactions impact the company's results so that their direction is psychologically aligned with the temperament of their executive team.

Dysfunctional boards that blindly insist on specific organizational design or tactics have been the source of many an avoidable upheaval.

Chief Executive Officer Temperament

The Nimble CEO's KPI is *mission accomplished* and their domain is *choicemaking, vision,* and *culture.* They fill the archetypal role of Sovereign as Chief Vision Maker and Chief Decision Maker.

They are responsible for forming and communicating the appropriate elements of the vision to the rest of the team. They are responsible for setting, installing, and maintaining the culture, which defines how the vision is executed. They become the executive coach for the top players to help them execute the vision.

> A NIMBLE EXECUTIVE HAS MORE ON THEIR "TO THINK" LIST
> THAN ON THEIR "TO DO" LIST.

For a commercial business executive, the mission is increasing shareholder value, determined by the business model with a KPI of some blend of *profit* and *growth*. Often, when highly profitable, they don't have to grow much, and conversely, if they are growing like crazy, they don't have to make much profit.

In non-profits, government, and education, it's about *accomplishing the mission* that's been mandated for the organization or agency.

The nimble CEO's noble purpose is to hold the vision and direct the culture that manifests the vision. Their deepest concerns are the wellbeing of their community. Their highest intention is to improve everything possible. Their motivators include personal impact and lasting legacy.

Their role is *strategic*, bounded by the organization's *what* objective and *why* rationale, under the guidance of the Board of Directors or their stakeholders.

CEOs have the longest planning timeframe in their organization, looking *three to five years* into the future, and preferably longer – even as long as 50 to 100 years into the future.

CEOs search for improvements in *efficiency* because this allows them to increase profits from the same level of sales and to grow without additional capital investment, or to accomplish their mission with fewer resources.

Today, *flexibility* and *Nimbility* have become extremely important in adapting and adjusting to rapidly changing market conditions, fluctuating demands from government, and changes in the quality of education and skills their personnel come to them with and without.

A CEO's risk profile shows that they can *accept risk* because they are creating a future that does not yet exist by using methods that have not yet been invented. Risk-averse executives don't last long in today's chaotic business conditions; they're outrun and outgunned by those who can manage, mitigate, and profit from risk.

They *set budgets* by orchestrating their resources to accomplish their mission.

They *consume* data to make executive decisions around how to best achieve their objectives, *monetization* for commercial organizations and *mission accomplished* for non-profit, government, and education.

They want *topsight* (the 30,000-foot view of where they are) and *foresight* (where they want to go) to make intelligent and defensible decisions, relying on data provided by the rest of their team.

> EVEN THE BEST GPS CAN'T OFFER GUIDANCE UNTIL IT KNOWS WHERE YOU ARE AND WHERE YOU WANT TO GO.

As Choicemaker, they must be able to *decide* with a high degree of effectiveness. They want to feel *confident* about their decisions in the face of rapidly changing market and field conditions.

In terms of communication style, CEOs tend to be flexible enough to effectively communicate with the temperaments of each of their diverse team members. Yet their own natural constellation tends to blend General, Match, Options, Internal, Proactive, and Toward.

In summary, the CEO has *low resistance* to new ideas and new technology. They are willing to consider disruptive technology when it has true potential to deliver outcomes that advance their mission.

See a summary of the key temperament dimensions in Figure 11. The **bold** font indicates that they embrace change.

	Objectives		Priorities				Criteria		
Title Domain	**KPIs**	**Role**	**Time Frame** (years)	**Risk**	**Budget**	**Data**	**Know**	**Do**	**Feel**
CEO Vision & Culture	**Mission** Accomplished **Profit &** **Growth**	**Strategic:** **What &** **Why**	**3-5**	**Accept**	**Set**	Consume, Monetize	Topsight, Foresight	**Decide**	**Confident**

Figure 11: CEO Temperament Profile. **Bold** = Embraces Change.

Chief Operating Officer Temperament

The Nimble COO's typical KPIs are *profits and losses (P&L)* and *customer satisfaction.* Filling the archetypal role of Chief Warrior, they ensure that things get done well.

Their domain is physical *assets,* all the tangible elements required to operate the company and how they are organized into a system to produce the product or service.

Since they are responsible for production, they also are responsible for customer satisfaction based on product quality, cost to produce that impacts pricing, product availability, delivery logistics, and remedial repairs under warranty.

They also oversee the customer experience through user experience dimensions, packaging, and training, by working closely with marketing to meet visual brand standards and ensure consistency in delivering on the marketing promise.

They are responsible for collaborating and communicating with the deployment team. They are responsible for architecting, procuring, installing, directing, and maintaining the physical systems, all of which define how the mission is accomplished. In companies that don't have an R&D department, they are also responsible for new product development. They become the executive coach for their management team to help them execute the plan.

> THE COO DESIGNS AND RUNS A WELL-OILED PRODUCTION MACHINE.

The nimble COO's noble purpose is to lead the production team to excellence, creating competitive advantage. Their deepest concerns are the consistency and efficiency of the operation. Their highest intention is to improve everything possible for best P&L performance. Their motivators include personal excellence and operational excellence.

Their role is a blend of *strategic*, bounded by the organization's *what* objective and *why* rationale, and *sequence*, determining the best tactical operating order.

COOs have a mid-range planning timeframe in the organization, generally looking *one to three years* into the future as they determine technology demands and customer expectations. (If they also have R&D responsibilities, this necessitates them looking longer into the future.)

COOs search for improvements in *efficiency, flexibility*, and *Nimbility* because this allows them to increase profits and customer satisfaction, and to expand without additional capital investment.

A COO's risk profile shows that they are *risk aware*. They weigh the known and certain of today's operation against potentially disruptive changes that improve desired outcomes. They are willing to consider the risk versus reward of changes to their process for even small reductions in cost because they know many tiny numbers add up to big numbers.

They *set budgets* by orchestrating their resources to accomplish their mission.

They *consume* data to make executive decisions around how to best achieve their objectives and *monetize* data for improving P&L and operating margins. Members of their team create data for the COO's consumption.

They want to *control the process* through *visibility*, relying on current data provided by the rest of their team.

They want to feel *certain* about their decisions because they must deliver the desired outcome without fail.

In terms of communication style, COOs need to be flexible enough to clearly communicate with the temperaments of each of their diverse team members (as well as with the executive team). They tend to have a natural constellation of a balanced, blended view leaning towards these characteristics: General, Mismatch, Procedure, External, Proactive, and Toward. They direct team members with the opposite styles to balance the details and deliver process stability.

In summary, the COO has *some resistance* to considering new ideas and new technology in relationship to a stable operation. They are willing to consider disruptive technology only when they see that it can realistically deliver improved outcomes that advance their mission.

See a summary of the key temperament dimensions in Figure 12. The **bold** type indicates areas where the COO embraces changes, and the Roman type (the technical term for ordinary, nonbold, nonitalic type) indicates areas where they accept change.

	Objectives		Priorities				Criteria		
Title Domain	KPIs	Role	Time Frame (years)	Risk	Budget	Data	Know	Do	Feel
COO Assets	**P&L, C Sat**	**Strategic, Sequence**	1-3	Aware	**Set**	Consume, Monetize	Control Process, Visibility	Efficiency	Certain

Figure 12: Chief Operating Officer Temperament Profile.
Bold = Embraces Change. Roman = Accepts Change.

Chief Sustainability Officer Temperament

Filling the function of the Chief Financial Officer plus much more, the Nimble CSusO[8] archetypal role is Chief Steward. They keep the company sustainable, viable, stable, and scalable. This is exemplified by directing cash

---

[8] We use the acronym *CSusO* (say it See Suss Oh) to differentiate the Chief Sustainability Officer from CSO typically referring to a Chief Security Officer or Chief Sales Officer, both T-Suite roles.

flow, making capital available for nimble innovation investment, legal compliance, and securing the company assets.

While the traditional CFO has been mostly a tactical historian, controlling and reporting the financial transactions of the company, the nimble CSusO fills a strategic role that focuses on architecting sustainable operations and growth. They accountably delegate to their team essential tactical financial functions such as cash flow management, balancing accounts payable with accounts receivable, capital raising, creditor management, and compliance oversight. This frees them to create sustainable growth and scaling systems strategy with checks and balances to steward key resources.

> ### THE CHIEF SUSTAINABILITY OFFICER OVERSEES CORPORATE STABILITY AND THE PATH FOR NIMBLE GROWTH.

The CSusO KPIs include *Company Stability* as measured by cash flow dynamics and asset risk index (including compliance status), and *Nimble Growth Readiness* as measured by financial assets & reserves and deployable resources. Yes, these are new KPIs, which are essential for installing Nimbility in the C-Suite.

We comprehensively review the execution risks that the CSusO must consider and manage in our companion book *The Nimble Company*.

The nimble CSusO's noble purpose is to oversee the stewardship of financial and physical assets. Their deepest concerns are sustainable financial operations, protecting company assets and funding future growth. Their highest intention is to provide the financial and physical means to manifest the vision and scale for sustainable growth. Their motivators include accuracy and providing a sage financial stability and growth perspective.

They're responsible for directing the funding *sequence*, allocating funds by the month or quarter, directing *when*, *where*, and *how much* money becomes available. Their planning timeframe tends to be *one to three years* out (multiple budget cycles). The exception to this is when planning for real estate and multi-year capital investments, which demand longer planning cycles.

CSusOs are *risk aware*, willing to consider risk versus reward payoffs. While they prefer to choose the conservative route, they'll take calculated risks when they see the right policies, guarantees, assurances, insurances, and due diligence, all of which are part of their asset risk index.

When it comes to budgets, they're responsible for *setting* budgets and *auditing* how people spend money within business rules. They consider the cash flow impact of a purchase as much, if not more than, the overall cost and return on investment (ROI).

When it comes to data, their job is to *create* and *mine* data to generate reports for the CEO. They also *consume* data as they plan for nimble growth. To make this happen, they must work with *accurate*, current data to extract *insight*, because the CSusO's role is to support the CEO's choicemaking and vision and provide the cash flow and asset *control* and future funding to make it happen.

They make decisions based on feeling *comfortable*. You've probably heard financial sages say, "I'm not comfortable with this." Or "I'm comfortable with these numbers."

In terms of communication style, CSusOs tend to be focused on the specific style that supports their role as Steward. They tend to have a natural constellation of these characteristics: Specific, Mismatch, Procedure, External, Proactive, and Away.

The CSusO's temperament means they have *medium resistance* to change and new ideas; they only agree when they are satisfied that the plan can upgrade cash flow, profit, compliance, or security.

See a summary of the key temperament dimensions in Figure 13. The **bold** type indicates areas where the CSusO embraces changes, with the Roman type indicating areas where they accept change, and *italic* type indicating resistant to change.

	Objectives			Priorities			Criteria		
Title Domain	**KPIs**	**Role**	**Time Frame** (years)	**Risk**	**Budget**	**Data**	**Know**	**Do**	**Feel**
CSusO Money	Company Stability, Nimble Growth Readiness	Strategic Sequence	1-3	Aware	**Set** *Audit*	Create, **Mine,** Consume	**Insight, Accurate**	*Control*	Comfortable

Figure 13: Chief Sustainability Officer Temperament Profile.
Bold = Embraces Change. Roman = Accepts Change.
Italic = Resists Change.

Chief Integrity Officer Temperament

The role of the Chief Integrity Officer or CintO[9] has been usually filled by the founder who embraced a servant leadership style, desiring to grow the team's skills and personal development as part of their vision and mission. They fill the archetypal role of Lover.

They serve the company by systematically increasing awareness at all levels about human factors and challenging thought processes and decisions that are going to undermine human factors, to the detriment of the company on every possible level: culture, productivity, profitably, and reputation. They focus on the company being profitable but not at the expense of the human and social responsibility reputation factors.

The CIntO won't tolerate moochers, entitlement mentality, victim mindset, learned helplessness, or resistance to accountability. Nor do they tolerate empathy deficits or reluctance to be challenging.

Being aware of the gap between what new team members need and what they haven't been taught, they identify required training for both essential skills (communication, collaboration, conflict resolution, accountability, etc.) and tactical skills (required to fulfill the role and responsibility). They implement the training and monitor use and effectiveness, making necessary adjustments to maximize team performance.

---

[9] We use the acronym of *CIntO* (say it See In To) for the Chief Integrity Officer to distinguish this role from the widely used acronym CIO as Chief Information Officer, which we place in the T-Suite.

The CIntO's typical KPIs are around employee engagement (leading), collaboration effectiveness (current), and brand perception (lagging). Their domain is *Walking the Talk*, insuring optics and culture alignment to deliver brand integrity: the company does what it says it does. They focus on *applied integrity*, integrity in action, not integrity as a concept or value, but integrity as a set of behaviors and values: embodied values, enacted values, and applied values.

Their tactical team may include:

- ❑ Chief Personnel Development Officer (CPDO) – this part of the traditional CHRO role oversees the following functions. The other part of this role (legal compliance) is a Stewarding role. If the company is large enough to warrant it, the CPDO might have directors who are direct reports:
  - o Chief Engagement Director – hiring, onboarding, individual accountability, and performance
  - o Chief Training Officer – collaboration effectiveness, team performance improvement, and accountability
  - o Chief Culture Officer – culture installation and protection at every point and layer of the organization.
  - o Chief Wellbeing Officer – ensuring employee physical health, mental health, and life balance.
- ❑ Chief Reputation Officer – brand perception and integrity, including public relations, customer experience development, monitoring, and maintenance, as well as media relations. This person coordinates closely with the Chief Marketing Officer for tactical deployment, who falls under the domain of the CRO.

Some companies might choose to combine oversight of employee engagement, training, culture, and wellbeing into a single Chief Personnel Development Officer.

The nimble CIntO's noble purpose is to love, in a compassionate love of humanity sense. If they're not coming from that place, it's not going to work. They balance *Challenge* and *Nurturance* described on page 70. Challenging is about drawing people into their best self. Nurturance is about support and emotional safety, acknowledgement, and blessing. Their deepest concerns are brand/culture misalignment & *Brand Slaughter*,[10] low engagement & low performance, and high conflict & divisiveness, resulting in an impaired team. Their highest intention is for each person to be expressing meaningful portions of their own life purpose through their role, without sacrificing their personal wellbeing or cherished relationships, plus each individual and team being clear about their true value to the company's success, and the company being clear about its true value to its customers and to society, which defines *vertical integrity alignment*. Their motivators include peak performance and peak actualization of human potential, happiness, and positive impact.

The CIntO always has the CEO's back in ensuring that no executive or managerial decisions run afoul of the company's defined integrity dimensions. This brings cultural alignment and stability to the S-suite and T-Suite so that stated values trickle down through the entire company.

---

[10] It's no surprise why David Corbin's great book, *BrandSlaughter* was a Wall Street Journal bestseller.

Their role is a blend of *strategic*, bounded by the organization's *what* objective and *why* rationale, and *sequence*, determining the best tactical operating order: get the right people in, onboarded, trained properly, accountability to make sure the training is used so there's effective collaboration.

Ultimately, they are responsible for the *legacy* outcome of the company.

CIntOs must be time frame fluid. They must think long-term about how the culture is to function and what it is to actualize when the company is mature, they must track what's happening today and what needs to develop in the near-team, and they must remain aware of the organization's mid-range planning focuses. In other words, the CintO looks *Current to 20 years* into the future as they determine the legacy culture, while paying attention to what's happening today, and what development is required to achieve the lasting cultural impact.

CIntOs search for improvements in effectiveness in walking the talk. They seek ways to improve employee selection, onboarding, retention, succession, training, accountability, supporting a healthy culture with a solid reputation which improves competitiveness and truly improves profits.

A CIntO's risk profile shows that they are *risk aware*. They see risks in the dimensions of their domain and reduce the risk of each aspect of their role. Yet they are willing to risk change to improve employee engagement, cultural effectiveness, and brand integrity.

They *set budgets* by orchestrating their resources to accomplish their mission.

They *create* data structures and measurements, and *consume* data to make executive decisions around how to best achieve their objectives. They *monetize* the data by making adjustments to team effectiveness and brand perceptions based on the data. Members of their team create data for the CIntO's consumption.

They want to know that they align and optimize performance and reputation, and they want to feel delighted wellbeing.

In terms of communication style, CIntOs need to be flexible enough to clearly communicate with the temperaments of each of their diverse team members as well as with the executive team. They tend to have a natural constellation of a balanced, blended view leaning towards these characteristics: General, Match, Options, Internal, Proactive, and Toward. They catalyze team members with the opposite styles to balance the details and deliver process stability. And, as needed, they facilitate optimal collaboration among the executive team.

In summary, the CIntO has *resistance* to considering new ideas and new technology that could conflict with culture and reputation, while remaining willing to embrace disruptive technology when they see that it can realistically deliver improved outcomes that advance the mission.

See a summary of the key temperament dimensions in Figure 14. The **bold** type indicates areas where the CIntO embraces changes, the Roman type indicating areas where they accept change.

Objectives			Priorities				Criteria		
Title Domain	KPIs	Role	Time Frame (years)	Risk	Budget	Data	Know	Do	Feel
CIntO Walking the Talk	Engagement, Collaboration, Brand Perception	Strategic & Sequence	0-20	Aware	**Set**	Create, Consume, Monetize	Align Performance & Reputation	Optimize Performance & Reputation	**Delighted Wellbeing**

Figure 14: CIntO Temperament Profile. **Bold** = Embraces
Change. Roman = Accepts Change.

Chief Revenue Officer Temperament

In the new nimble organization, the Chief Revenue Officer is responsible for all activities that generate revenue,
including R&D and overseeing marketing and sales. This
keeps the business transformation (Magician) activities
under one strategic officer.

> THE NIMBLE CRO GENERATES MARKET DEMAND
> AND DELIVERS PROFITABLE TRANSACTIONS
> THROUGH MEANINGFUL PRODUCTS.

We are discussing the role from the nimble viewpoint
versus the traditional view of the CRO who is responsible
for sales and marketing, which now moves to the T-Suite
and is filled by a chief of sales and chief of marketing
who report to the CRO.

To be clear, we view sales as personal actions taken to
facilitate a transaction, while marketing is non-personal
actions taken to facilitate a conversation with sales or
trigger a transaction.

The CRO strategically balances the need for new technology with the need to serve the current desires and requirements of customers so a healthy revenue flow is maintained. See Figure 15.

Figure 15: The CRO Value Creation Continuum — An Example of Non-siloed Communication and Collaboration Across the Revenue Generation Functions

This blend of activities can create a seamless customer experience from awareness to purchase, yet we've seen that the strengths of most CROs lean heavily toward either sales or marketing. Few CROs are equally wise in marketing, sales, and R&D.

This challenge is solved with tactical chiefs skilled in each of these areas who collaborate and communicate to fill the gap by assigning sales responsibility to a VP of sales or a chief sales officer, and marketing responsibility to a VP of marketing or a chief marketing officer, and R&D to a VP of product development or chief of R&D.

A CRO's KPIs include the number of *leads* and lead quality, *sales* and margin (the gross profit on a sale), and customer *loyalty* as determined by customer longevity, meaning the products serve the market. The challenge is that sales is a short term KPI, marketing (lead generation) is a medium term KPI, and customer loyalty (product development) is a long term KPI. Placing this with a single strategic officer who oversees these tactical details brings a unified balance to these mission critical activities.

CROs tend to *accept* risk because the revenue function requires continuous testing and tweaking of product development, marketing messages and methods, as well as expanding sales territories and entering new markets.

The nimble CRO's noble purpose is to oversee all elements of current and future revenue generation. Their deepest concerns are competitive wins. Their highest intention is to provide a consistent, predictable flow of revenue. Their motivators include effectiveness and winning.

The CRO's role is the *strategic* deployment of product development, marketing, and sales systems, with chiefs designing the systems and VPs focusing on *how* to achieve the outcome and *who* will do the job.

Their planning timeframe tends to be a mix of long-term, *three years* for product development, and short term, *a year or less*, because sales results are measured monthly.

They can set their budget for balanced product development, marketing, and sales activities. This helps solve the innovators dilemma of blindly pursuing a technology that no longer has a viable market.

Their role is to *create, consume,* and *monetize* the data, generating market information, deciding how to approach the marketing, gathering, and analyzing sales data, and directing product development, identifying the most effective path to revenue.

The CRO must know *the customer,* how to *connect* with them, and how to *convert* relationships into sales. They prefer to feel like they're *winning* or *successful.*

CROs focus on the specific communication style that supports their role. They tend to have a natural constellation of these characteristics: Specific, Match, Procedure, External, Proactive, and Toward.

CROs have *low resistance* to change because they recognize the need to be constantly testing methods to increase revenue, because the market is constantly in flux.

See a summary of the key temperament dimensions in Figure 16. The **bold** type indicates areas where the CRO embraces changes, with the Roman type indicating areas where they accept change.

	Objectives		Priorities				Criteria		
Title Domain	**KPIs**	**Role**	**Time Frame** (years)	**Risk**	**Budget**	**Data**	**Know**	**Do**	**Feel**
CRO Revenue	Product, Leads, Sales	Strategic Sequence	0-3	**Accept**	Set	Create, Consume, Monetize	The Customer	Connect, Convert	Winning, Success

Figure 16: Chief Revenue Officer Temperament Profile.
Bold = Embraces Change. Roman = Accepts Change.

The S-Suite Temperament Comparison

Compare the temperament of the key strategic officers in the S-suite (Strategic Suite) in the following table. This helps you understand their key world view differences, so you can become a better leader by providing insights that communicate the information that each team member needs so they can excel in their role. See Figure 17.

The Nimble C-Suite

Title Domain	Objectives			Priorities				Criteria		
	KPIs	Role	Time Frame (years)	Risk	Budget	Data	Know	Do	Feel
Chief Executive Officer Vision & Culture	Mission Accomplished, Profit & Growth	Strategic	3-5	Accept	Set	Consume, Monetize	Topsight, Foresight	Decide	Confident
Chief Operations Officer Assets	P&L, Customer Sat	Strategic Sequence	1-3	Aware	Set	Consume, Monetize	Control Process, Visibility	Efficiency	Certain
Chief Sustainability Officer Money	Company Stability, Nimble Growth Readiness	Strategic Sequence	1-3	Aware	Set Audit	Create, Mine, Consume	Insight, Accurate	Control	Comfortable
Chief Integrity Officer Walking the Talk	Engagement, Collaboration, Brand Perception	Strategic Sequence	0-20	Aware	Set	Create, Consume, Monetize	Align Performance & Reputation	Optimize Performance & Reputation	Delighted Wellbeing
Chief Revenue Officer Revenue	Product, Leads, Sales	Strategic Sequence	0-3	Accept	Set	Create, Consume, Monetize	The Customer	Connect, Convert	Winning, Success

Figure 17: S-Suite (Strategic Suite) Officer Temperament Comparison. **Bold** = Embraces Change. Roman = Accepts Change.

The T-Suite, the Tactical Officers

The next executive temperaments we'll consider move to the tactical side of the operation. While they'll be tapped for strategic insights, most of their time is invested in tactical delivery. These executives are your Tactical Suite or *T-Suite*.

Chief Product Officer Temperament

A CPO's KPIs include new *product cadence* – the rhythm that new products come to market – and *manufacturability* – how well can the products be produced with requisite quality. Responsible for R&D (research and development), they work closely with marketing and sales to understand what customers want now and in the future, as

{ 133 }

meets the company's mission. They also explore technology that can bring new, transformation products to market in alignment with the company's vision.

CPOs *accept* risk since they are responsible for exploring innovations to existing products and ultimately producing completely new products that serve the company's target market. They balance this risk acceptance with risk awareness as they develop products that can be reliably manufactured.

> THE NIMBLE CPO IS RESPONSIBLE FOR INNOVATING PRODUCTS
> WHICH BRING NEW VALUE TO THE MARKET
> THAT CAN BE PROFITABLY MANUFACTURED AND SOLD.

The nimble CPO's noble purpose is to oversee socially conscious product development that brings transformational value to the target market. Their deepest concerns are understanding what brings true value to the company's TBL/ESG purpose. Their highest intention is to provide a consistent, predictable flow of new products. Their motivators include team innovation effectiveness, recognition of their contribution to the company's success, and product legacy.

The CPO's role is overseeing the *tactical* deployment of product development, focusing on *how* to achieve the outcome and *who* will do the job. They work with the CRO on strategy and product futures to align with the company's mission. They also work with the COO to create products that can be consistently manufactured at the target price point.

Their planning timeframe tends to be time fluid, *six to thirty-six months* because product development is a blend of meeting current needs with what will bring competitive value down the road. They clearly understand the three key future horizons discussed on page 90, so have a six to 36 month forward looking timeline.

They can only *spend* their budget, having to solicit approval for any expenditure above their signature limit.

Their role is to *consume* and *monetize* the data, analyzing market information, deciding how to approach the product development, analyzing research data, identifying the most effective path to market success, and directing their team on executing the plan.

The CPO must know how to *innovate*, so that they can nimbly *create valuable products* that uniquely satisfy the market.

They like to feel like they're *certain*, and they feel this way when they're maximizing the impact of their R&D budget and creating no-fail products.

CPOs focus on a specific communication style that supports their role. They tend to have a natural constellation of these characteristics: Specific, Mismatch (because they must create flawless products), Options, Internal (because payoff is often way down the road), Proactive, and Toward.

CPOs have *low resistance* to change because they are magicians who transform the market with their product innovations.

See a summary of the key temperament dimensions in Figure 18. The **bold** type indicates areas where the CPO embraces changes, with the Roman type indicating areas where they accept change, and *italic* type indicating resistant to change.

Objectives			Priorities				Criteria		
Title Domain	KPIs	Role	Time Frame (years)	Risk	Budget	Data	Know	Do	Feel
CPO **Product**	Product Cadence, Manufactur -ability	Tactical, Sequence	0.5-3	**Accept**	*Spend*	Consume, Monetize	**Innovate**	**Create Valuable Products**	Certain

Figure 18: Chief Product Officer Temperament Profile.
Bold = Embraces Change. Roman = Accepts Change.
Italic = Resists Change.

Chief Marketing Officer Temperament

A CMO's KPIs include the number of *leads* and lead quality, and market *positioning*. They oversee market research and competitive research, as well as physical brand compliance (look and feel), messaging strategy and deployment (including what guarantees are required for perceived risk reduction), and gathering market data for product development. They are responsible for tactical deployment of brand-based public relations in collaboration with the Chief Reputation Officer, who reports to the Chief Integrity Officer.

CMOs tend to be *aware* of risk since they are responsible for the return on the marketing investment, and this requires continuous testing of marketing messages and methods.

> THE CMO IS RESPONSIBLE FOR CREATING PROSPECTIVE AND CURRENT CUSTOMER CONVERSATIONS, WHETHER ONLINE OR IN PERSON.

The nimble CMO's noble purpose is to oversee driving relevant conversations with prospective and existing customers. Their deepest concerns are getting and holding customer attention. Their highest intention is to provide a consistent, predictable flow of relevant conversations. Their motivators include effectiveness and recognition of their impact on the company's success.

The CMO's role is overseeing the *tactical* deployment of marketing systems, focusing on *how* to achieve the outcome and *who* will do the job.

Their planning timeframe tends to be short, *a year or less*, because marketing results are measured monthly although the long-term impact of marketing activities is cumulative. It takes time to get a new prospect to become aware and act.

They can only *spend* their budget, having to solicit approval for any expenditure above their signature limit.

Their role is to *create, consume,* and *monetize* the data, generating market information, deciding how to approach the marketing, analyzing sales data, and identifying the most effective path to market success.

The CMO must know *the customer*, be able to *connect* with them and *inspire action* to have a sales conversation.

They like to feel like they're *effective*, and they feel this way when they're maximizing the impact of their marketing budget.

CMOs focus on a specific communication style that supports their role. They tend to have a natural constellation of these characteristics: Specific, Match (unless they're editing), Procedure, External, Proactive, and Toward.

CMOs have *moderate resistance* to change because they are willing to test methods to increase revenue, yet they often require data before agreeing to make a change.

See a summary of the key temperament dimensions in Figure 19. The **bold** type indicates areas where the CMO embraces changes, with the Roman type indicating areas where they accept change, and *italic* type indicating resistant to change.

Objectives			Priorities				Criteria		
Title Domain	**KPIs**	**Role**	**Time Frame** (years)	**Risk**	**Budget**	**Data**	**Know**	**Do**	**Feel**
CMO Customer	Positioning, **Leads**	*Tactical, Sequence*	0-1	Aware	*Spend*	*Create, Consume, Monetize*	**The Market**	**Connect, Inspire Action**	**Effective**

Figure 19: Chief Marketing Officer Temperament Profile.
Bold = Embraces Change. Roman = Accepts Change.
Italic = Resists Change.

Chief Sales Officer Temperament

A CSO's KPIs include *sales* and *margin* (the gross profit on a sale). This is accomplished through an effective sales organization, whether inside sales, field sales, or reseller partner channels. They may be responsible for online sales or catalog sales, although this is often assigned to a marketing officer. The margin KPI indicates how well their team sells value, negotiates with customers, and re-sists unnecessary discounting.

CSOs tend to *accept* risk because the revenue function requires continuous expanding sales territories and entering new markets. Pursuing the unknown always carries perceived risk.

The nimble CSO's noble purpose is to oversee an effective sales operation. Their deepest concerns are competitive wins. Their highest intention is to provide a consistent, predictable flow of high margin sales. Their motivators focus on winning.

The CSO's role is the *tactical* deployment of sales systems and activities, focusing on *how* to achieve the outcome and *who* will do the job.

Their planning timeframe tends to be short, *a year or less*, because sales results are measured monthly.

They can only *spend* their budget. This means they must solicit approval for any expenditure above their signature limit.

Their role is to *create, consume,* and *monetize* the data, gathering and analyzing sales data, and identifying the most effective path to high margin revenue.

> ### THE CSO ORCHESTRATES PROFITABLE TRANSACTIONS.

The CSO must know how to *compel the right prospects* to be able to *close* sales by aligning the product to the customer's requirements and desires.

They like to feel like they're *winning*, and this is often a very different feeling from other executives.

CSOs focus on a specific communication style that supports their role. They tend to have a natural constellation of these characteristics: General, Match, Options, External, Proactive, and Toward.

CSOs have *low resistance* to change because they are willing to test methods to increase revenue.

See a summary of the key temperament dimensions in Figure 20. The **bold** type indicates areas where the CSO embraces changes, with the Roman type indicating areas where they accept change, and *italic* type indicating resistant to change.

	Objectives			Priorities			Criteria		
Title Domain	KPIs	Role	Time Frame (years)	Risk	Budget	Data	Know	Do	Feel
CSO Sales	Sales, Margin	*Tactical*	*0-1*	**Accept**	*Spend*	Create, Consume, Monetize	Convince the Customer	**Close sales**	**Winning**

Figure 20: Chief Sales Officer Temperament Profile.
Bold = Embraces Change. Roman = Accepts Change.
Italic = Resists Change.

Chief Information Officer Temperament

A CIO's KPI is just one thing, and this thing only: *uptime*. As long as the data processing system is up, running well, and secure, so is their career. If the system goes down and this results in major business impact, their career is over.

For this reason, they are *risk averse*. They will want to avoid anything that might cause a security or system issue. As a result, with every new technology under consideration, they will require proof of concept and a meticulous deployment strategy.

The nimble CIO's noble purpose is to oversee the stewardship of data assets. Their deepest concerns are operating loss of I.T. system functions and data theft. Their highest intention is to provide the data required to manifest the mission. Their motivators include security and providing a reliable I.T. platform.

The CIO's role is the *tactical* deployment of business systems, focusing on *how* to achieve the outcome and *who* will do the job.

Their planning timeframe tends to be short, *a year or less*, because many of them operate in a reactive mode. Because of this they only plan for the next annual budget cycle. CIOs who plan for longer time spans tend to be the exception.

They can only *spend* their budget, which means they must solicit approval for any expenditure above their signature limit. The only way they get more money is in an emergency, and that's likely to be a career-limiting event.

Their role is to *curate* and *manage* the data, with no real focus on the data themselves. This is a tactical mistake on the part of many CIOs, since they can provide valuable strategic insights through intelligent data analysis.

Therefore, they want to know that the data and system is *safe*, and therefore they're safe. To do this requires *visibility* into all aspects of the data systems, both under their direct control and outsourced services.

What they'd prefer to do is *innovate*, yet this is almost impossible without executive air cover and a sandbox that allows them to safely play with new technologies.

They like to feel *invisible*. Mark got this insight at 36,000 feet from the CIO of a large pharmaceutical company with data centers in 65 countries. After four glasses of red wine in first class, he revealed that his top goal was being invisible. "When they notice me, I'm in trouble," he lamented. This position has been confirmed over and over again by other CIOs.

CIOs focus on a specific communication style that supports their role. They tend to have a natural constellation of these characteristics: Specific, Mismatch, Procedure, External, Reactive, and Away.

Is it any wonder that CIOs have *high resistance* to new technology and don't find many of the value propositions of current technology attractive? It's just not worth risking their career to consider anything that's not tried and true. This changes in a nimble organization.

See a summary of the key temperament dimensions in Figure 21. The **bold** type indicates areas where the CIO embraces changes, with the Roman type indicating areas where they accept change, and *italic* type indicating resistant to change.

Title Domain	Objectives			Priorities				Criteria		
	KPIs	**Role**	**Time Frame** (years)	**Risk**	**Budget**	**Data**	**Know**	**Do**	**Feel**
CIO Data	*Uptime*	*Tactical*	*0-1*	*Averse*	*Spend*	*Curate, Manage*	*Safe,* **Visibility**	Innovate	*Invisible*

Figure 21: Chief Information Officer Temperament Profile.
Bold = Embraces Change. Roman = Accepts Change.
Italic = Resists Change.

Chief Human Resources Officer Temperament Dilemma

For reasons discussed on page 69, we recommend splitting the CHRO into two separate roles: the CCO (Chief Compliance Officer) and the CPDO (Chief Personnel Development Officer).

This is because the traditional CHRO's responsibilities require wearing two incompatible hats: policy enforcement, which is the domain of the Steward, and talent development (engagement, training, and culture), which is the domain of the Lover.

Typical CCO Stewardship KPIs can include candidate requisition open-to-fill time, monitoring policy infractions, benefits management, and employee online reputation compliance. These CCO responsibilities fall squarely in the CSusO's strategic domain.

> ## To motivate good performance:
> ## Trust and Verify

A note on employee termination: we call this *collaborative disengagement*, discussed on page 183. This is done by the CCO in consultation with the CIntO and whoever has been doing that employee's performance reviews, and after legal review.

Typical CPDO Lover KPIs are related to the employee experience: onboarding (designed by the CIntO), development, and conflict resolution. These CPDO responsibilities fall squarely in the CIntO's strategic domain.

With talent often being the most expensive part of the business, including recruiting, wages, benefits, termination costs – and worst case, employee lawsuit settlement costs – both the Steward-oriented CCO and the Lover-oriented CPDO are *risk averse*, avoiding anything that might cause a personnel or legal issue.

Their combined noble purpose is to minimize personnel upheavals. The CPO's deepest concerns being infractions that create legal dilemmas, and the CPDO's deepest concerns being people issues that disrupt individual performance, team collaboration, or culture wellbeing.

The nimble CPDO's noble purpose is to oversee the stewardship and development of talented people. Their deepest concerns are poor candidate selection, poor onboarding and engagement, poor collaboration, and personnel dealing with life issues that impair work performance. Their highest intention is to select, nurture and challenge people to manifest the vision by excelling in their role and on their team. Their motivators are actualizing human potential.

The nimble CCO's noble purpose is to oversee the stewardship of the company through policy enforcement. Their deepest concerns are employees being out of integrity with their agreements and behaving outside of cultural boundaries and legal limits as defined by policy. Their highest intention is to guide those who infract policy back to the agreed-upon norms. Their motivators are being just and keeping the company safe.

The CPDO's role is the *sequential* and *tactical* procedures surrounding employment, with a focus on *how* to achieve the mission outcome and *who* will do the job. The CCO's role is *tactical*, focused on verifying policy compliance and managing corrective action.

The CPDO's planning timeframe tends to be mid-range, *a year or two*, because they must plan for attrition and team growth. Ideally, they oversee succession planning in cooperation with the executive team.

Whereas the CPO is in-this-moment tactically managing compliance, with a planning time frame of a year or less, usually about consulting with the CEO, CSusO, and CintO about adjusting policy to reflect changes in technology, legal mandates, and culture.

Both can only *spend* their budget, which means they must solicit approval for any expenditure above their signature limit.

Their role is to *create* and *consume* employee data to implement staff development policies and accountability procedures. Ideally, they'll consume data to determine best hiring and training practices.

> THE NIMBLE **CPDO** IDENTIFIES AND DEVELOPS THE COMPANY'S MOST EXPENSIVE RESOURCE, TALENT.
> THE NIMBLE **CCO** KEEPS THAT TALENT ALIGNED WITH POLICY.

The CPDO wants to know the executive team's *goals*, required *team* talent, and deployment *sequence,* so that they bring in the right talent at the right time for the right scope of work. They like to *develop* talent and *facilitate* team growth. They like to feel *engaged* and *collaborative.*

Conversely, the CCO wants to know the *goals* of the policy and the *policy* itself. They want to *monitor* and *enforce* the policy. They like to feel that they are *just* in their decisions and actions.

CPDOs focus on a specific communication style that supports their role. They tend to have a natural constellation of these characteristics: Specific, Match, Procedure, External, Proactive, and Toward.

In contrast CCOs tend to have a natural constellation of these characteristics: Specific, Mismatch, Procedure, External, Reactive, and Away.

Notice how these conflicting, yet necessary, communication styles make it virtually impossible for one person to fill both roles.

CPDOs are *open to* change because personnel, team, and culture development is constantly in a state of ongoing upgrades. In contrast, CCOs have *some resistance* to change because of the highly procedural nature of their role with policy-driven decisions.

The nimble CPDO's and CCO's role is to *create* data to document their choices and *consume* employee data with an eye toward early identification and correction of procedural and policy infringements, and hiring practices.

Is it now clearer than ever why traditional HR officers and directors have characteristically lived in a perpetual state of distress? Dividing their responsibilities in archetypally wise ways is the solution to this nagging problem.

See a summary of the key temperament dimensions in Figure 22. The **bold** type indicates areas where the CPDO and CCO embrace changes, with the Roman type indicating areas where they accept change, and *italic* type indicating resistant to change.

The Nimble C-Suite

	Objectives			Priorities			Criteria		
Title Domain	KPIs	Role	Time Frame (years)	Risk	Budget	Data	Know	Do	Feel
CPDO **Recruit** **Team**	Recruit, Develop	*Tactical*	0-2	*Averse*	*Spend*	Create, Consume	**Goals,** **Team,** **Sequence**	**Develop,** **Facilitate**	Engaged, Collaborative
CCO **Verify** **Team**	Monitor & Enforce Policy	*Tactical*	0-1	*Averse*	*Spend*	Create, Consume	**Goals,** **Policy**	**Monitor,** **Enforce**	Just

Figure 22: Chief Personnel Development Officer and Chief
Compliance Officer Temperament Profiles.
Bold = Embraces Change. Roman = Accepts Change.
Italic = Resists Change.

The T-Suite Temperament Comparison

T-Suite officers hold essential, critical roles that are primarily tactically focused. Comparing how each one's
worldview differs, and how the T-Suite's overall
worldview differs with the C-Suite's worldview, can immeasurably boost your leadership communication and
direction. See Figure 23.

Objectives			Priorities				Criteria		
Title Domain	KPIs	Role	Time Frame (years)	Risk	Budget	Data	Know	Do	Feel
CPO Product	Product Cadence, Manufactur-ability	*Tactical,* Sequence	0.5-3	**Accept**	*Spend*	Consume, Monetize	Innovate	Create Valuable Products	Certain
CMO Customer	Positioning, Leads	*Tactical,* Sequence	0-1	Aware	*Spend*	Create, Consume, Monetize	**The Market**	Connect, Inspire Action	**Effective**
CSO Sales	Sales, Margin	*Tactical*	0-1	**Accept**	*Spend*	Create, Consume, Monetize	Convince the Customer	Close sales	Winning
CIO Data	Uptime	*Tactical*	0-1	Averse	*Spend*	Curate, Manage	Safe, **Visibility**	Innovate	Invisible
CPDO Recruit Team	Recruit, Develop	*Tactical*	0-2	Averse	*Spend*	Create, Consume	Goals, Team, Sequence	Develop, Facilitate	Engaged, Collaborative
CCO Verify Team	Monitor & Enforce Policy	*Tactical*	0-1	Averse	*Spend*	Create, Consume	Goals, Policy	Monitor, Enforce	Just

Figure 23: T-Suite Tactical Officer Temperament.
Bold = Embraces Change. Roman = Accepts Change.
Italic = Resists Change.

The Implementer Temperament

The final temperament group is the implementers: the people who utilize the tactics that the T-Suite has selected and "sequentialized" in order to accomplish the strategies that the S-Suite has embraced on behalf of the company's vision, mission, and goals.

The more tactically oriented a management role is, the more their temperament must be one that focuses on current KPIs, such as production, leads processed, and current sales. Implementers tend to have very short time horizons: days, weeks, quarters, as appropriate for their roles. They tend to be risk averse, spend budgets, and curate or create data. They want to know how to accomplish their tasks, they want to end their day with tasks complete, and they want to feel appreciated and safe.

Chapter Summary

- ❑ Each member of the executive team has a unique, required temperament that makes them highly suitable for their roles and responsibilities, increasing Nimbility.
- ❑ This alignment allows each executive to effortlessly work within their zone of genius to execute their responsibilities.
- ❑ Misaligned roles and temperaments decrease resilience and innovation, and trigger avoidable upheavals.
- ❑ Understanding these temperamental differences brings psychological savvy to the executive team, engendering respect and appreciation for their colleagues' perspective.

Ask Yourself

- ❑ Thinking about each of the roles of my executive team, how well aligned are they with the necessary temperament?
- ❑ What executives are out of temperament alignment?
- ❑ If I could bring alignment of temperament to role, what impact could that have on my leadership effectiveness and the company's performance?
- ❑ Is my company better served by resolving the inherent conflict built into the CHRO role by splitting it into a CCO role and a CPDO role?

Ask Your Team

- ❑ Do you feel that your temperament suits your position for highest effectiveness, or do you feel a different role would suit you better?
- ❑ Where do you see misalignment of talent and temperament within your team that when adjusted would improve your leadership effectiveness and team performance?

Action Plan

- ❑ Review the roles of your team for temperamental alignment.
- ❑ Train your executives about desired role temperaments so that they can understand each other and the members of their teams.
- ❑ Plan for how you'll adjust roles with temperament for greater Nimbility.
- ❑ Bring in help if you feel this task is too complex or unclear. We can help.

Chapter 6:
Executive Nimbility Skills

Now that you have a better understanding of executive temperament – the mindset of success for each role – let's look at the skillset required across the board for Nimbility.

Nimble leadership isn't just the ability to direct good people; it's the intention and skills required to operate a sustainable, scalable, and profitable business. The more complex your offering, the more potential upheavals you'll face,[11] which in turn means that your success will require your leadership skills to become more sophisticated than most training and experience offers.

Ninety percent of commercial CEOs come from a sales background.[12] While this can be extremely valuable because business success is directly related to sales success, executives with this background require training in leaderships mindset and skills that they likely have not yet received.

---

[11] We discuss in depth the sources and resolutions for upheavals in our companion book, *The Nimble Company*.
[12] Reported in Anthony Parinello's excellent book, *Selling to Vito*.

Ultimately your leadership success doesn't hinge on how much you know or how well you can sell, but on how you play well with others.

"Eighty five percent of your financial success is due to your personality and ability to communicate, negotiate, and lead. Shockingly, only 15 percent is due to technical knowledge" according to the Study of Engineering Education, Charles Riborg Mann, published in 1918 by the Carnegie Foundation. This century-old observation is still true today. It was shocking then because the assumption was knowledge is the source of success. While knowledge matters, it's not even close to being enough.

> GOOD PEOPLE RARELY FOLLOW SMART JERKS.

Master Seven Critical Executive Skills That Enable Nimbility

In working with leaders of all types over the past decades, we've identified seven skills required for sustainable executive success. When one skill is weak or missing, trouble follows. The good news: these skills can be developed and improved.

What follows is a discussion of the nimble executive skill stack that goes far beyond requisite knowledge needed to competently create strategy and execute tasks. Like application developers and software programmers must have a skill stack to create valuable, effective, and usable code, an executive must have certain skills to run a sustainable, scalable, profitable, and ultimately salable organization. Usually referred to as soft skills, we call these hard-core soft skills *Essential Skills*.

Read on to identify if you and your team have these skills and to assess where you need to strengthen them.

1. Presence

Presence is that certain something that attracts people, commands their attention, and permits a leader to engage. Presence provides the ultimate in first impressions. Without it, you don't even get a chance to lead, even when you have a position of authority.

Presence is a powerful combination of emotional intelligence (EQ) plus authentic personal integrity that creates charisma. People can fake presence for only so long before they are recognized as mostly fake image and little substance. That's a recipe for unsustainable leadership. Contrast this with the sustainable leadership formula that Elvis Presley observed: "Image is an introduction to substance."

> IF YOU CAN'T AUTHENTICALLY GAIN AND HOLD THEIR ATTENTION, YOU CAN'T LEAD THEM.

Summarizing the observations of organizational researchers, 35 percent of your success is because of your EQ and 50 percent because of your cognitive capacity (IQ), and 15 percent is your knowledge. Emotional intelligence (EQ) is the ability to integrate heightened awareness and management of yourself, of others, and of situations and things. Cognitive capacity is the ability to handle complexity, roughly measured by IQ.

When you're unaware of others, you're a narcissist. When you're unaware of things, you're a minimalist.

When you're unaware of situations, you're impact illiterate. When you're unaware of yourself, you're a self-neglectful altruist. A nimble leader must be able to presence themselves to all of these awareness dimensions and integrate these in service to sound decision-making.

Without this dimension of integrity, you're doomed. Once customers and your team discover that you're not of your word, or not as you appear to be, you've blown their trust in you. The game is over, forever.

Purpose-paradigm alignment and *self-sovereignty* are the oft-overlooked foundations that make presencing – the persistent awareness of shared humanity – possible.

Purpose-paradigm alignment happens when you sculpt your worldview, selfview, and sense of meaning in life to best support your purpose. This, in turn, is what fundamentally guides your choices about what to execute. The particulars of how to elevate your capacity for purpose-supportive paradigm sculping go beyond the scope of this book. Contact us if you seek this kind of training.

Self-sovereignty requires becoming masterful at self-regulation. Self-regulation includes self-responsibility, reptile brain management & emotional literacy, and *tensions competence*, which is the ability to find wisdom in the seeming complexity of both/and instead of finding false assurance in the over-simplicity of either/or. We discuss these topics deeper in the companion book *The Nimble Company*.

Purpose-paradigm alignment and highly developed self-sovereignty are so important because of the capacity for presencing that these skills create, which determines your cognitive capacity, which controls how you execute.

{ 154 }

Here's what we mean: the less purpose-paradigm alignment and self-sovereignty one has, the more distressed and chaotic one becomes. The more distressed and chaotic one becomes the less capable of presencing they are. In the absence of strong presencing muscles, the capacity to think things through in deep ways becomes deeply impaired.

Ask yourself: On a scale of one to ten, how is your ability to integriously command attention? Which of these dimensions of EQ – purpose-paradigm alignment or the various components of self-sovereignty – requires upgrading in you?

2. Personal Control

While most of us would love to be free spirits, unbound by convention and routine, a nimble leader knows how to be free and unbound within the wisdom of mature stewardship.

Personal control, sometimes called self-discipline, requires personal and professional routines. It's within that structure that we paradoxically find freedom to focus on the variables that nimble leaders manage.

For example, Steve Jobs, arguably one of the most effective and disruptive businessmen in recent times, wore a uniform of black mock turtleneck, blue jeans, and New Balance sneakers. This meant he had one less thing to think about. He also had a meditation practice that kept him centered and effective. (He also had other EQ deficits that limited him as a leader.)

> A LEADERS MOST VALUABLE RESOURCE IS COGNITIVE CAPACITY,
> WHICH IS SUPPORTED BY DIET, EXERCISE, AND REST.

Without a personal routine, you'll skip meals, not get enough sleep, and not get the exercise you need. The self-deprivation that an insufficient personal routine creates directly impairs your most valuable resource as a nimble leader: your cognitive capacity.

Without a personally controlled routine, you'll fight fires all day long and never attend to the critical strategies, sequence prioritization, and customer attention.

Ask yourself: Does your daily routine maximally support your resourcefulness? Does your routine ensure that every aspect of what is required for optimal wellbeing gets consistent attention?

3. Foresight

The nimble executive constantly has an eye on the future because a central part of your role is to predict the future so you can lead through upheavals. Nimbly resourceful executives become futurists who anticipate and then craft wise versions of what will come by constantly refining their methods of insight and discernment.

> THE BEST WAY TO PREDICT THE FUTURE IS TO INVENT IT.
> – BUCKMINSTER FULLER

When was the last time you did a future vision exercise? In today's highly accelerated rate of change, if it wasn't within the past thirty days, you may face a looming disaster and don't yet see it.

Why? Because, as Scott Adams puts it, "Goal thinkers only see what's between them and the goal line. Systems thinkers avoid slow moving problems." Scott points out the big difference between being tactical (working to the goal) and being strategic (creating a system that scores goals).[13]

Foresight is how we engineer systems that generate value for our customers. We must look beyond our customers' time horizon to continuously delivering value that's consistent, sustainable, scalable, and profitable.

NIMBLE LEADERS PREDICT SELF-FULFILLING PROPHECIES.

Your S-Suite in particular must have a long-range vision of the future, with the CEO having the longest-range view. They also must have a keen sense of sequencing savvy: the ability to determine what needs to be done before something critical can be executed with the least friction and the greatest efficiency. This doesn't merely apply to tasks. It also applies to macro decision-making, such as which initiatives need to be underway before others can be maximally worthwhile to undertake, what kinds of personnel, opportunities, and advisors need to be pursued before others can be maximally beneficial.

Ask yourself: What is your vision horizon? If it's not at least ten years out, you're on a downward path. When was the last time you revisited your vision? If it's not in the last thirty days, you're developing a blind spot.

---

[13] Read Scott Adam's excellent book, *How to Fail at Almost Everything and Still Win Big.*

4. Business Acumen

Most executives have a strong skillset in one area of business acumen: their expertise.

Yet, when working with your strategic and tactical team, you need to understand how their part of the business works to apply Nimbility to their roadmap. You need business acumen to understand their motivations and how to satisfy their needs.

A nimble executive understands how all the elements of business fit together so they can speak the language of every player in the organization. Without business acumen, you'll always be viewed as a stuffed suit. Here's a synopsis of business acumen:

The Seven Business Pillars

1. **Products** that create unique value for the target market
2. **Marketing** that triggers relevant conversations
3. **Sales** acumen that facilitates mutually profitable transactions
4. **Service** that earns customer loyalty
5. **Operations** that scale with economic cycles
6. **Finance** that controls cash flow and funds the future
7. **Culture** that upholds a unique brand experience.

Ask yourself: On a scale of 1 to 10, how proficient are you with each of the seven business pillars? Where do you need to improve your acumen? How can you get tutoring in the elements of that pillar?

5. Communication Skills and Collaboration Competence

A nimble executive must be able to communicate ideas and actions clearly, aligned with how their counterpart receives communication. Then they must judiciously use humor.

We've found that most leadership breakdowns are rooted in under-developed communication skills, especially in difficulty adjusting communication style to the person and issue at hand. (Discussed earlier starting on page 94, an in-depth description of the skills that are necessary for this also goes beyond the scope of this book. We stand ready to assist.)

Nimble executives take responsibility to communicate in the way that works for the people they lead. That's often different from the executive's natural way of communication.

Here is one of many examples of this. Some people need to *speak in order to think* while others need to *think in order to speak*. Both styles are equally valid yet can be misinterpreted by those unaware of this. For instance, if you speak in order to think, your team may mistake your perspective exploration as direction. If you think in order to speak, they may mistake your dead air as incompetence or uncertainty.

These are examples of legitimate temperament differences and mental processing styles that nimble leaders need to become fluent with to communicate and collaborate effectively.

In addition, each role in your organization requires a right-matched approach to processing information. For example, a CFO needs to be detail oriented and by the rules, while the marketing team wants to be flexible and creative. Do you see how they each require a different approach to communication and conversation?

> **SPEAK AND WRITE WELL BECAUSE CLEAR COMMUNICATION HAS MORE VALUE THAN ANY PHYSICAL TASK YOU CAN DO.**

For example, when asked, "How does it work?" there are times to say, "It works great!" – a classic sales response – and there are times when you've got to deliver the nitty-gritty details. Being specific when your team wants the big picture incites boredom, so err on the side of less detail, trusting that if they want specifics, they'll ask for more details.

Collaboration competence and impact literacy are also foundational skills that go hand-in-hand with effective communication.

Collaboration competence goes far beyond saying you believe in the virtues of collaboration. For a nimble leader, this requires a very specific set of skills, not only to participate in high performance, high happiness collaboration, but also to consistently facilitate this, and to get collaboration back on track when inevitable breakdowns occur.

Impact literacy is absolutely vital for nimble leaders to create an *accountability-capable* culture. As mentioned earlier in this book, because of the deteriorated state of society and education, very few otherwise competent personnel arrive at the doorstep of our business with well-developed impact literacy.

If you don't train them in the four integrated skills of collaborative accountability (accountability-capable commitments, best practices upgrades, implementation breakdown repair, and frequent growth-oriented performance reviews), their ability to assess cause-and-effect (the foundation of impact literacy) will always undermine your culture's execution ability and productivity. We discuss these skills on page 180.

When it comes to judicious use of humor, a savvy executive knows that well-crafted humor brings a team together. Personal attack or group belittling humor has no place in a nimble company. Healthy humor releases tension, offers a light-hearted perspective about a problem's impacts so it can become easier to solve, and makes the insanity of a no-longer useful viewpoint easier to accept.

Scott Adams has written more than 10,000 jokes about corporate ridiculousness in his Dilbert® cartoon. He has probably done more to systematically reduce corporate idiocy than any leadership expert. Elon Musk has been known to say in a meeting, "…this could be a Dilbert cartoon."[14] to humorously point out a problem.

When we authentically find something funny and laugh together, that joyful experience shows that we are, in that moment, in agreement about deeper concerns and higher intentions. Nimbility is full of laughter and joy.

---

[14] "I love Dilbert! Use it all the time to illustrate that we're doing something wrong at Tesla/SpaceX if it could be a Dilbert cartoon irl. This happens more often than I'd like (sigh)." Elon Musk, Twitter, 12/15/2021.

> ## AN EXECUTIVE WHO LAUGHS A LOT
> ## LEADS A TEAM THAT LAUGHS A LOT.

We've observed that when someone says something funny in a staff meeting, the team looks to the executive for the cue on whether to laugh, or not. If you hear something you think is funny, if you agree with it, and if you view it as a healthy expression of humor, we recommend that you laugh out loud to give permission for your team to laugh, too.

Ask yourself: How often do you have problems with your team getting your message? If it's more than rarely, it's time to work on understanding of how people communicate. How often do your people seem blind about the positive and negative impacts of their words and actions on others? If it's more than rarely, it's time to work on impact literacy and how people optimally collaborate. How are you using humor in your leadership to release mental Nimbility in your team?

6. Persuasion Skills

To lead nimbly, you must persuade your team to align their priorities with your priorities and take action that they may not have taken on their own. This requires non-coercive persuasion and synergistic negotiating skills so agreements get created that all involved want to keep. We talk more about this with accountability-capable agreements on page 180.

Executives negotiate every day: with vendors, employees, bankers, customers, lawyers, politicians, their spouse and kids, and each other. The better you are at synergistic negotiation, the more profitably you can run your business.

> ### THE BEST NEGOTIATIONS END WITH AN AGREEMENT THAT BOTH SIDES WANT TO KEEP.

Ask yourself: How frequently do you find yourself agreeing to things that you really don't want? How often do you think that you could have kept more margin and the other party would still be happy? How often do you feel that you could have been more persuasive? If it's not rare, consider a course or mentoring in synergistic negotiation skills or learn ethical persuasion skills.[15] How often do you only find out only after someone's reliability went to Hell in a handbasket that they really resent the agreement you negotiated with them? If it's not uncommon, consider a course or mentoring in synergistic negotiation skills and ethical use of personal power.

7. Makes Resourceful Decisions

Nimble executives are comfortable with uncertainty. They initiate actions without knowing the complete roadmap because they have a decision-making system based on a combination of business rules and intuitive guidance that leads to more resourceful decisions than bad decisions.

---

[15] For more on the topic, see Mark S.A. Smith's book, *Guerrilla Negotiating* written to provide the antidote for the dirty tricks customers use to take the profit out of your deals.

The result is efficient allocation and management of resources, such as time, personal energy, imagination, cognitive capacity, people, and money.

Resourceful decisions are based on a combination of the prior six skills discussed here, plus a strategy that effectively considers the decision elements. The best executives use a checklist to ensure that the critical elements get considered during the decision process.

You might be thinking, "I only need to trust my gut to make decisions." This isn't scalable and it doesn't facilitate succession plan implementation, because unless you're unusually talented and your people are unusually gifted, you can't teach others how to trust their gut anywhere near as easily as you can help them learn how to develop a comprehensive decision checklist. Your gut might be the final test, but it's not the only test.

Equally important is knowing when to decide. Making a decision too early may be undermined by *confirmation bias*, where one cherry picks data to support their decision, potentially heading the wrong direction in the light of new knowledge. Waiting too long misses opportunity windows. Decide when a decision is due, then start collecting information and insight to draw upon when it's time to choose.

> A NIMBLE EXECUTIVE KNOWS THAT THE PATH OFTEN BECOMES CLEAR AFTER THEY EMBARK ON A JOURNEY TO A NEW DESTINATION.

Often, you won't know the path to your destination until you begin, which is why an explorer on an expedition sends forth a scout to find a path before directing forward the rest of the company. Or they hire a local guide who knows a path.

When asking for input from your team, we suggest using the words, "I want to understand your perspective..." instead of "I need your advice..." Why? Because people expect for you to heed their advice, but usually are less attached to decisions based on their perspective. This avoids the, "They never follow my advice, so I'm just going to keep my thoughts to myself..." mindset that leads to withholding important information, triggering unnecessary upheavals.

Ask yourself: Do you have a decision-making checklist that you routinely use and refine? If not, time to build it and show others how to build and refine theirs.

How Did You Do with Your Assessment?

Be honest with yourself, as you're the only person to benefit. Now that you've identified where you need to build your executive strengths, put together your personal plan to make it happen.[16]

Chapter Summary

❑ We've identified seven key executive skills for Nimbility, as follows.

---

[16] If you want to work on any of the skills we have covered in this chapter, consider attending our Nimbility Skills Summits, and leave with your own customized Monday-ready action plan. We can also conduct a summit specifically tailored for your team. NimbilityWorks.com/summit

❑ Presence: emotional intelligence and authentic personal integrity. If you can't get their attention and build trust, they won't follow you.

❑ Personal Control: the self-discipline of personal and professional routines, including self care, which supports your most valuable resource, your cognitive capacity.

❑ Foresight: the ability to see the future because the executive's job is to lead the team where customers will spend money in the future.

❑ Business Acumen: knowledge of how the key components of business systems work, so that you don't abdicate accountability and lose control.

❑ Communication Skills and Collaboration Competence: the ability to communication to your team and individuals in a way that they understand, so that you're responsible for clear communication and effective collaboration.

❑ Persuasion Skills: the ability to negotiate and lead people to understand and embrace your position.

❑ Makes Resourceful Decisions: the capacity to know how to decide and when to decide.

Ask Yourself

❑ On a scale of one to ten, how is your ability to integriously command attention? Which of these dimensions of EQ (purpose-paradigm alignment and the various components of self-sovereignty) requires upgrading in you?

❑ Does your daily routine maximally support your resourcefulness? Does your routine ensure consistent attention to every aspect of what is required for optimal wellbeing?

❑ What is your vision horizon? If it's not at least ten years out, you're on a downward path. When was the last time you revisited your vision? If it's not in the last thirty days, you're developing a blind spot.

❑ On a scale of 1 to 10, how proficient are you with each of the seven business pillars? Where do you need to improve your acumen? How can you get tutoring in the elements of that pillar?

❑ How often do you have problems with your team getting your message? If it's more than rarely, it's time to work on understanding how people communicate.

❑ How are you using humor in your leadership to release mental Nimbility in your team?

❑ How often do your people seem blind about the positive and negative impacts of their words and actions on others? If it's more than rarely, it's time to work on impact literacy and how people optimally collaborate.

❑ How frequently do you find yourself agreeing to things that you really don't want? How often do you think that you could have kept more margin and the other party would still be happy?

❑ How often do you feel that you could have been more persuasive? If it's not rare, consider a course in synergistic negotiation skills or learn ethical persuasion skills.

❑ How often do you find out only after someone's reliability went to Hell in a handbasket that they really resent the agreement you negotiated with them? If it's

not uncommon, consider a course in synergistic negotiation skills, ethical use of personal power, and accountability-capable agreements.

❑ Do you have a decision-making checklist that you
routinely use and refine? If not, time to build it and
show others how to build and refine theirs.

Ask Your Team

❑ What skills do you feel could be improved to increase
your personal effectiveness?

❑ What would it be worth to do that?

❑ What would it cost if you didn't?

❑ Would you be willing to be part of a regular executive skills development course?

Action Plan

❑ Create your plan for executive skill building, both for
yourself and for your team because the nimble executive never stops skills development which compound
over time to create leadership superpowers.

Chapter 7:
Upgrades Required Before Deploying a Nimble C-Suite

Before you can deploy a nimble C-Suite, you'll need to make sure your team possess basic Nimbility skills and you have procedures in place to let them use those skills to the greatest effect.

If you and they don't have these skills or systems, it will be difficult to form and lead a nimble C-Suite.

Upgrade Your Team

Your team most likely requires upleveling of their personal Nimbility skills, those elements that bring them consistent Nimbility. There are four key Nimbility components:

❑ Mindset – how your team thinks, the temperament lens they use to view their world, and the mental resources they use to make decisions

❑ Skillset – your team's ability to perform strategic and tactical tasks to optimally fulfill their role and responsibility

❑ Toolset – the models, policies, software, reports, systems, processes, and procedures that enable your team to efficiently deliver their required results.

{ 169 }

❑ Habitset –behaviors that don't require conscious thought which lead to resourceful outcomes.

Complete this upleveling with mentoring and coaching that ensures skills integration into daily routines.

Uplevel to a Nimble Mindset

Let's take a closer look at team mindset as defined by their perspective lens. Our worldview is set by our experiences, training, culture, personal norms, religious or spiritual practices, and mental health.

For example, a narcissist has a warped lens about their personal importance, while one who is arrogant resists other viewpoints because they are afraid of losing status when they are proven wrong. A sociopath doesn't care about the wellbeing of others and insists that the end justifies the means – a viewpoint that enlightened consumers consider repugnant, especially for a socially responsible company.

Promote a Fluid Perspective Lens

Being nimble requires intentional fluidity with your perspective lens because a rigid lens has blind spots. Understanding the lenses of your team brings their perspective into sharp focus that enables you to tap into their diverse perspectives to extract a broader range of wisdom than you alone possess. While each role demands a specific lens for daily operations, the ability to envision through other lenses brings powerful understanding, and access to new unrealized resources.

Encourage your team to regularly take on their peers' perspectives as part of the decision-making process. This brings a broad-perspective mindset to all key team members, which results in the ability to consider options that may have previously been unthinkable.

While this may be a challenge for some, if this level of maturity is beyond a particular executive, that person doesn't belong in the C-Suite, or perhaps they belong in the T-Suite but not the S-Suite. Yes, it will be easier for those who have had true debate training, where arguing the opposite side of the issue is de rigueur.

Once your team experiences lens fluidity, they become open to upleveling their skills.

Be Soft on People, Hard on Tasks

The Harvard Negotiation Study found that the most effective outcomes happened when leadership was soft on people and hard on tasks. We discuss this on page 66.

Soft on people doesn't mean indulging them but seeing that although they may have best intentions, they may have insufficient training or an incomplete perspective for consistent success. They aren't bad people; they just have a disconnection between their good intentions and their impacts. They need training, redeployment to a role more suitable to their skills, or, if they are unable to align intentions and impacts, employment with another company.

Hard on tasks means that all team members have accountability-capable agreements about their role and responsibility. There are defined consequences for missing deadlines or quality standards. There is a defined remediation path to correct the missed goal. And no one gets a pass, not the CEO or a founder's relative.

Balance Transformation with Stability

Do so without the expense of one or the other, because transformation without stability breeds chaos, and stability without transformation breeds stagnancy and status quo addiction.

Clearly Understand and Effectively Implement Principles, Policies, and Procedures

Principles, policies, and procedures connect strategy to tactical implementation, so an organization consistently walks its talk.

Principles are the universal guidelines that support a nimble organization. Every team member requires training in your core principles and how to correctly use them. Guiding principles for decision-making provide a framework that equips your people to turn your company's values into wise choices within their scope of authority and responsibility, especially during upheavals.

A *policy* is a set of guidelines that outline the organization's plan for tackling various issues. An effective policy outlines what employees must do or not do, directions, limits, and guidance for decision making. Policies are set by the executive team, with sub-policies set by management teams. Becoming policy-heavy kills motivation, engagement, and culture. Reserve policies for hard limits on behaviors with legal ramifications, such as physical and data security policies. For everything else, rely on guiding principles for decision-making guidance.

A *procedure* explains a specific, detailed tactical action plan for carrying out a principle or policy. It shows employees step-by-step the who, how, and when to deal with a situation. This becomes critical during upheavals when less experienced employees aren't equipped to make cogent choices in chaos. This avoids the two a.m. problem: what seems reasonable under stress at two in the morning looks dumb in the cold morning light.

Key Skills Training for Collaboration Nimbility

This book has guided you through the many elements to consider, both strategically and tactically, when building a nimble executive team. You probably have identified areas where your team needs upgrades.

Key areas to consider:

❑ Identity development – Does everyone on your team have a self-concept that supports their role, responsibility, and authority? Do they see themselves as nimble, confident, humble, resilient, innovative? Does their behavior reflect their necessary identity? What unresourceful identity elements do they need to outgrow, such as overreliance on a specific leadership style?

❑ Mindset development – Mindset follows identity. Mindset is also impacted by corporate and personal culture, assigned KPIs, and the lens on their role and responsibility. Does each team member's mindset completely support their KPIs, role, and responsibility?

❑ Skillset development – Do all of your team members have the leadership, communications, negotiating, decision-making, analytics, and technical skills required for their role?

❑ Toolset development – What tools do each of your team members need to build or master to deliver peak performance? Do any of them resist using new tools?

❑ Habitsets – Do you have team members who need mentoring or coaching to consistently integrate their skills into daily activities? Do they need an accountability partner to keep them focused on their growing edge and prevent them from reverting to old, unresourceful behaviors?

The fastest path is with outside, professional help. Identify who can diagnose and prescribe upgrades for individuals on your team, and for your team as a whole. This investment will pay dividends for a lifetime.

Create a Blindspotting Culture

In gymnastics and at the gym when lifting, you have a spotter whose responsibility is your safety. They are there so you can attempt new moves or lift heavier weights that are outside your comfort zone. They make your expansion safe.

This same principle applies to your team's troubleshooting, innovation, and exploration. A way that everyone can have each other's back is to blindspot ideas so everyone remains safe. (If you are familiar with the psychological concept of "shadow", you already know about the harmful consequences of unrecognized and unaddressed blind spots.)

In nimble cultures, everyone on your team is a spotter who shares responsibility for safety. This stability helps make it safe to create outside the lines. It's safe to leave your comfort zone because you have spotters that keep you safe.

If you think about this in terms of the core archetypes we covered (starting on page 60), this is an example of the necessary counterbalance between the Magician (transformation) and the Steward (stability) archetypes.

What Being a Spotter Is and Isn't

A spotter doesn't gossip, snitch, tattle, shame, blame, manipulate, isn't arrogant or judgmental, and doesn't seek revenge, carry out vendettas, or act like a victim. They aren't a self-appointed savior or enforcement agent. And they aren't someone who breaks confidentiality by divulging private information publicly or by telling others something that was said to them in confidence.

Rather, a spotter is someone who cares deeply about an organization's success, about developing or maintaining a healthy company culture, and about elevating brand integrity. When a spotter detects a possible blindspot that could be harmful to success, culture, or brand, they offer that information to someone who will be able to make wiser decisions with that information than without it.

How to Be a Spotter

Here are five steps in being a truly helpful spotter:

- ❑ Remember that everyone in a company is a spotter because all humans have blind spots, and a sign of maturity to be receptive to the illumination of potential blind spots.
- ❑ Commit to being a blindspotter who abstains from doing this in harmful ways like those listed at the start of this section. In other words, choose authentically noble motives.

❑ Before bringing a potential blindspot to someone's attention, make sure you select the right person to bring it to – someone who will be able to make wiser decisions with that information than without it – and that you're in a heartset of love.

❑ Inform your chosen person about the potential blindspot in private and without shame or blame. Also let them know your deepest concerns about the harm this blind spot might cause and your highest intentions about the positive things that could come from illuminating this blind spot, so they are fully clear about the noble reasons you're bringing this to them.

❑ Let go of attachment to outcomes. A spotter's role is to offer information that might be unrecognized, not to be in charge of decisions that are made as a result of providing that information.

Spotter Team Training

Becoming a truly helpful spotter requires not only the willingness to do blindspotting on behalf of an organization's wellbeing, but the willingness of the organization and all of its leaders to be blindspotted. Establishing this willingness and becoming adept at truly helpful blindspotting often requires training, since most people have never been taught how to do this in good ways. As adept blindspotters and blindspotting trainers, we stand ready to help.

The Upleveled Whistleblower

In the traditional context, whistleblowers exposed malfeasance or fraud, potentially subjecting them to repercussions and attack. In nimble organizations, whistle-blowers become valued blindspotters who bring important information to strategic and tactical decision-makers that might otherwise remain hidden, buried, or ignored by management.

Who might be a blindspotter in nimble organizations? Anyone! This is because in nimble organizations, transparency is a proactive antidote to unforeseen upheavals, and freely sharing information is part of the culture. With the whistleblower now reframed as a blindspotter, let's now expand on this to map an escalation path that shows blindspotters how to best route their information.

Establish a Clear Escalation Path

The right escalation path means that potentially critical information efficiently travels up the command structure without friction, blame, or shame, which keeps vital intelligence flowing to prevent, detect, or address potential upheavals. See Figure 24.

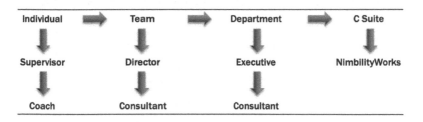

Figure 24: Define an Escalation Path for Information Flow and Access to Additional Skills

The individual who is part of a department team can question their supervisor. If the supervisor needs more skills, they can access a coach (either internal with the CIntO or external) for further development.

The supervisor can question their director. If the director needs more skills, they can access a consultant (either internal with the CIntO or external).

The director can question the executive, either vice president or chief officer. If the executive needs more skills, they can access a consultant (either internal with the CIntO or external).

The chief officer can question their peers or access an executive consultant or mentor.[17]

Adopt Lean Hierarchy Three-Level Leadership

Any time an organization needs to successfully navigate change, they would be wise to embrace the concept of three-level management and lean hierarchy.[18]

Lean hierarchy, the foundation of effective organizational design, evaluates current cognitive power and archetypal alignment at all levels of managerial leaders and matches each to the level of work complexity they can handle for maximum strategic, tactical, and task impact.

> THE DOMINANT, MOST PROFITABLE PLAYER IN ANY MARKET
> IS OFTEN OPERATING AT ONE COGNITIVE LEVEL HIGHER
> THAN ITS COMPETITORS IN KEY EXECUTIVE FUNCTIONS.
> – ELLIOTT JACQUES

---

[17] We at the NimbilityWorks are here to help. Let's talk. See page 219.

[18] Thanks to Chris Stark for alerting us to this technique.

Three-level leadership, the cornerstone of strategy execution, ensures that employees at every organizational level get two supporting and interacting managers:

1. A manager who is accountable for using fair and motivating managerial leadership practices with every direct report as described in the following section.

2. A mentor – the manager's manager – who ensures, through observation, that the manager is holding each direct report accountable for their work while adding value when needed.

This method rapidly installs new culture and processes in an organization that must change to succeed. It is also essential in creating a Nimbility culture.

Upgrade Your Communication and Collaboration Processes for Nimbility

Let's discuss what to upgrade in your approach to communication and team collaboration.

Employee Review and Upgrade Procedures

Conventional employee review processes tend to kill Nimbility, destroy culture, severely limit innovation, and hobble performance. They occur too infrequently (most commonly annually) and they typically focus on whether someone gets a raise, a promotion, or fired.

While those are important decisions, the primary purpose of performance reviews in nimble companies is personnel growth. Growth doesn't happen once a year. It unfolds continuously. This means that support and modification must occur regularly. That might mean every quarter, every couple of weeks, or something in between.

A person's role, newness to the role, and temperament determine how often these reviews need to occur.

Accountability-Capable Agreements Procedure

Four integrated accountability procedures ensure continuous executive, employee, and team development. They are:

- ❑ Accountability-Capable Agreements
- ❑ Best Practices Upgrades
- ❑ Implementation Breakdown Repairs
- ❑ Performance Reviews that include Collaborative Disengagement when appropriate.

In today's world, good intentions are substitutes for agreements or get treated as though they are agreements. This sets the stage for unnecessary conflict. When a good intention is a substitute for a commitment, nothing gets done even though everyone means well. When a good intention is treated like an agreement, everyone has a different idea about what the commitment entails, which leads to disappointments and a potential chain reaction of missed agreements. This causes unnecessary upheavals.

Accountability-Capable Agreements

An *accountability-capable agreement* procedure specifies three things: observables, attributes, and time frames.

- ❑ *Observables* are what an independent witness would see did or didn't occur
- ❑ *Attributes* are specifications about what resources are needed to get the task done and what constitutes excellence

❑ *Time frames* are determined after looking at sequencing: what needs to be done by whom, in what order, how long that step should realistically take, and who gets the handoff.

Agreements also include a commitment to provide immediate updates if complications arise that result in needing to revise the time frame.

All agreements are in writing to prevent misunderstanding about the nature of the agreement. This can be a simple email detailing the three elements discussed above.

Best Practices Upgrade Procedure

Nimble organizations regularly upgrade their best practices. The procedure for this has two steps: blessing what is going well and identifying "even better ifs."

Blessing what is going well means being specific about what going well means and why this is valuable. Calling out why it's valuable is a crucial component in impact literacy training.

People are more likely to do the right thing when they see their positive impacts when they do well, and they see their negative impacts when they don't. Only addressing the negative teaches people to operate from an *avoid* viewpoint instead of the desired *embrace* viewpoint.

"Even better ifs" enhance Nimbility instead of getting caught in gripe sessions that build bad feelings.

In this second part of the Best Practices Upgrade procedure, people brainstorm about how something could be done even better, the superior outcome this would create, and the benefits this outcome would provide.

Once brainstorming is complete, an elevated best practice gets selected, and this becomes an additional accountability-capable agreement that is added to each person's accountability-capable agreements list.

Implementation Breakdown Repair Procedure

Even with accountability-capable agreements and best practices upgrades, unexpected complications can still occur that cause breakdowns in agreement implementation or collaboration effectiveness.

When these breakdowns occur, they need to be dealt with in ways that lead to improved effectiveness and collaboration instead of lingering conflict and resentment.

The *Implementation Breakdown Repair* procedure is a four-step process for turning breakdowns into engagement, collaboration, and accountability upgrades. Here are those four steps that each person discloses:

❑ Their own unintended contributions to the breakdown

❑ The unintended negative impacts their unintended contributions had

❑ The impact repair they will do when a repair is feasible

❑ How they will handle future similar situations more effectively than they knew how to in the current situation.

That upgrade commitment is then recorded as another accountability-capable agreement. (It should be noted that training is usually required before Breakdown Repair procedures can be fruitfully conducted because of the groundwork that must first be done. We stand ready to provide your team with that training.)

Performance Review Procedure

The performance review session is conducted like a best practices upgrades session, except that the items that are reviewed are that person's or team's accountability-capable agreements, and whatever has been added to that list as a result of best practices upgrades sessions and breakdown repair sessions.

Performance reviews also include *growth edges*. The individual or team selects a top growth edge to focus on between performance reviews. During each review, progress with that growth edge is discussed and a plan for the next step, or a new growth edge, is agreed upon for discussion during the next performance review. Use the guidelines for accountability-capable agreements for specifying growth edge plans.

Collaborative Disengagement Procedure

Can you see the impact of integrating accountability-capable agreements, best practices upgrades, breakdown repair procedures, and performance reviews that focus on these, plus growth edges?

This approach helps people hold themselves accountable, and this in turn makes it clear when a raise, a promotion, or disengagement is called for.

Collaborative disengagement, as paradoxical as that term might sound, occurs when someone undergoing performance reviews shows a pattern of not completing agreements. This doesn't necessarily mean they are a bad person, or even a lazy person. What it always means, though, is that they are not right-matched to their role; collaborative disengagement is simply an acknowledgment that a wrong match exists between a person and a role. (It should be noted that conducting collaborative disengagement meetings well requires some training and also that these should only occur after consulting with your corporate attorney.)

When collaborative disengagement is necessary and is done well, this can have very positive company and community reputation impacts on online employee review sites such as GlassDoor.com.

The Plan for the Team Changes with Succession and Grooming Procedures

Team upheavals are inevitable and shouldn't be a complete surprise. People retire, choose a different life or career path, have family needs that drive job changes, experience extended illness, and occasionally unexpectedly pass away.

The upheavals-literate executive makes plans for promotions and succession, knowing that this is a necessary part of their routine strategy development. This includes ongoing training through the Chief Integrity Officer in corporate culture development, skill building, and perspective expansion. It means creating a corporate culture of learning, including personal and professional growth.

Nimble teams grow from within because they know that bringing in outside executives who are upheaval illiterate can slow them down or derail them entirely.

The Holographic Team Structure That Prepares People for Promotion and Succession

A nimble organization practices understanding the strategic components of each person's role and responsibility. They bring their experience and wisdom to decide the optimal sequence and optimal tactics to produce the desired and required outcomes.

This means that leaders at each level of the organization learn how to effectively use strategy, sequence, and tactics. By developing the practice and perspective required to view their departments as sub-businesses, they bring executive level thinking to their domain. This is what prepares them for succession without having to undergo significant retraining.

Avoid the Peter Principle

This holographic approach to promotion and succession reduces the probably of becoming trapped by the *Peter Principle*, in which people get promoted to their level of incompetence.

We see this not primarily as a personal capacity problem, but mostly as a perspective and training problem, a succession and grooming problem.

It most frequently happens when a tactician is promoted to a strategic role without the necessary training and coaching on how to shift their mindset to think and act strategically. They revert to tactical tasks because that's their comfort zone – where their rewards have come from – and hence can't effectively perform their new role. This scenario frustrates everyone involved.

The Peter Principle reigns supreme in companies with a broken HR system, where Petered-out people become human remains at their career's final resting place.

With all of this in mind, let's take a fresh look at how to prepare people for successful succession and confident career growth.

Vice President

The vice president is a focused strategist responsible for translating the overarching strategy of the Chief into sub-strategies for their department's functions. They are responsible for approving and overseeing the process tactics of their teams using nimble principles. While vice president roles are not necessary in smaller companies, they become essential when orchestrating multiple departments and multiple divisions in larger organizations. They make sure that nimble principles are properly deployed across diverse locations.

Director

The director is responsible for translating the overarching strategy the vice president has set into sub-strategies for their team functions. The director is responsible for orchestrating their teams to produce the required outcomes, and to fully understand how this supports the rest of the organization. They are ultimately responsible for directing the procedural tactics of their teams using nimble principles.

Team Leader

The team leader is responsible for implementing the sub-strategy through optimal sequencing in their team's tactical implementation through defined procedures.

How to Know What Your Team and Customers Will and Won't Accept Today

The *Nimbility Window* identifies how your team views the world in terms of their ability to nimbly adopt a new strategy, idea, action, market, etc. See Figure 25.

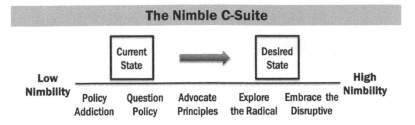

The Nimble C-Suite

Current State → Desired State

Low Nimbility | Policy Addiction | Question Policy | Advocate Principles | Explore the Radical | Embrace the Disruptive | High Nimbility

Figure 25: Nimbility Window, Moving the Team from Rigid, Low Nimbility to Disruptively Nimble

How to Use the Nimbility Window to Rapidly Implement New Ideas

We see the Nimbility Window as a powerful tool for executives to identify the attitudes and fears of their team and customer when applied to transformational ideas and actions. It illustrates the transition steps that cannot be skipped in bringing one from a low Nimbility state to a high Nimbility state.

If your team finds new ideas unthinkable because they are missing context, or because they are trapped in paradigm attachment disorder or inertia, you can implement a gradual change in culture, communication, and collaboration that gradually moves the Nimbility Window. Over time, entertaining disruptive ideas become less threatening and more intriguing.

It begins at the left in a low Nimbility state with *policy addiction*, where the executive team demands rigid compliance with existing policies designed to lock down any innovation or deviation from the currently held standard.

The path to increasing Nimbility demands that you *question policy* and accept that we outgrow what worked well in the past. Next you can move away from policy addiction to *adhering to principles*, which birth better guidelines instead of continuing rules that undermine a team's thought process or productivity.

Once your team is operating from nimble principles, they can *explore the radical* – concepts and ideas that would have been career challenging to bring up under a policy-addicted business. From there, your team can incrementally develop so it's able to *embrace the disruptive.* This brings high Nimbility and high Upheavals Literacy. We can help you plot this path based on your situation, your desired state of Nimbility, and the current state of your executives and culture.

Assessing Team Attitudes for Embracing Upheaval

We use the Nimbility Window to assess *attitudes, abilities,* and *actions* that need to be adjusted, and we use psychologically sound methods that can make it easier for your team and customers to willingly come along.

The following survey presents key ideas and asks for a response ranging from Policy Addiction to Embrace the Disruptive. For example:

Ask yourself the following global questions to get a sense of the Nimbility level of yourself and your team. Answer on a scale of one to five using these reference points.

1. I/They exhibit Policy Addiction.
2. I/They are willing to Question Policy.
3. I/They will Advocate Principles.
4. I/They are willing to Explore the Radical.
5. I/They are willing to discerningly Embrace the Disruptive.

Testing Nimbility of the Top: The CEO and the Board

"When it comes to your *board's* ability to listen to and consider ideas from you, which of the five ratings above most closely matches their typical response?" (Answer this question for each of your board members.)

"When it comes to *your* ability to listen to and consider an idea from your board members, which of the five ratings above most closely matches your typical response?

Average these numbers to identify the Nimbility between you and your board. Anything less than a three requires immediate attention because it indicates potential for unseen upheaval starting at the top of your organization.

Testing Nimbility of Your Executive Team

"When it comes to your *executives'* ability to listen to and consider ideas from you, which of the five ratings above most closely matches their typical response?" (Answer this question for each of your executive team members.)

"When it comes to *your* ability to listen to and consider an idea from your executive team, which of the five ratings above most closely matches your typical response?"

Average these numbers to identify the Nimbility between you and your executive team. Anything less than a three requires immediate attention because it indicates potential for unseen upheaval from your executive team.

Testing Nimbility of Your Management Team

"When it comes to your *management team's* ability to listen to and consider an idea from you, which of the five ratings above most closely matches their typical response?" (Answer this question for each of your management team members.)

"When it comes to your *management team's* ability to listen to and consider an idea from *their team*, which of the five ratings above most closely matches their typical response?" (Answer this question for each of your management team members.)

"When it comes to *your* ability to listen to and consider an idea from your management team, which of the five ratings above most closely matches your typical response?"

Average these numbers to identify the Nimbility between you and your management team. Anything less than a three requires immediate attention because it indicates potential for unseen upheaval from your management team.

Testing Nimbility of Your Front-Line Team

"When it comes to your *front-line team's* ability to listen to and consider an idea from you, which of the five ratings above most closely matches their typical response?" (Answer this question for each of your front-line team members.)

"When it comes to *your* ability to listen to and consider an idea from your front-line, which of the five ratings above most closely matches your typical response?"

Average these numbers to identify the Nimbility between you and your front-line team. Anything less than a three requires immediate attention because it indicates potential for unseen upheaval from your front-line team.

Now that you have an idea of how nimble your team is today, you can plot a path that brings them into a whole new era of Nimbility.

Chapter Summary

❑ You'll most likely need certain upgrades to your skills, and your executive team's skills, and to add certain Nimbility procedures before deploying your Nimble C-Suite.

❑ The three key Nimbility components are mindset, skillset, and toolset.

❑ Mindset includes understanding and matching temperament to role and responsibility. Upleveling mindset includes promoting a fluid perspective lens to broaden understanding.

❑ Skillset includes balancing nurturing with accountability, balancing transformation with stability, and developing critical collaboration competencies.

❑ Policy must reflect the new mindset and skillset use.

❑ Create a blindspotting culture to proactively prevent Nimbility blocks that trigger unnecessary upheavals. This includes an upleveled whistleblower culture that brings critical issues to management's attention without creating drama or damage.

❑ Upgrade procedures and agreements to bring authentic transparency and practical Nimbility to your team.

❑ Proactive succession planning and leadership grooming reduces the inevitable disruptions of team members departing.

❑ Use the Nimbility Window to identify how to lead the transformation.

❑ Assess team attitudes for embracing upheaval so you can determine where to focus attention and remediation.

Ask Yourself

❑ What personal upgrades are at the top of my list?
❑ What are the obvious upgrades to my team and what's at the top of the list?
❑ What policy changes need to happen to support the upgraded team?
❑ How can the impact of integrating accountability-capable agreements, best practices upgrades, breakdown repair upgrades, and performance reviews that focus on these, plus growth edges improve my Nimbility?
❑ How can it improve the Nimbility of my team?
❑ Where are the gaps in my succession planning and grooming? What needs attention now?

Ask Your Team

❑ Where do you see gaps in our mindset that limit our ability to be nimble?
❑ What's the impact of these gaps on our ability to perform our mission?
❑ Would you be willing to explore upgrades to our procedures that increase collaboration?
❑ Do you have a clear succession path for yourself and your team? Would you find it useful to have clarity in this path?

Action Plan

☐ Identify your personal upgrade plan: mindset, skill-set, toolset, and habitset.

☐ Perform the team assessment in the last portion of this chapter, as it will identify key blocks to Nimbility.

☐ Determine what upgrades are required to deploying a Nimble C-Suite.

☐ If you need assistance with your upgrades, contact NimbilityWorks to discuss how we can support and guide you on your journey. See page 219 for more information.

Chapter 8:
Your Plan to Deploy
a Nimble C-Suite to Make
Integrity Profitable

Now it's time to put your plan in action. You've considered the key points in this book. You've argued with yourself and debated your team on key trends and business issues and come to some conclusions. What's next?

Are You Willing, Able, and Ready?

What nimble upgrades do you need to consider before leading your team to Nimbility? Where do you need coaching and guidance? Until you're prepared to be a nimble leader, anything you do will bring frustration and failure. Of course, the alternative is slow decline and a limited legacy. Ask yourself:

❑ What are my motivations to lead the transformation to a Nimble C-Suite?
❑ What happens if I choose to maintain the status quo?
❑ What challenges do I foresee leading the Nimble transformation?

What's Your New Nimble Vision?

Once you're ready, create your vision for your Nimble team. Ask yourself:

❑ What is the executive team structure I see as most nimble for my vision and mission?

❑ How do my executive team align with the archetypally correct roles?

❑ Where are there gaps in my leadership team's capacities? Do I have people who might fill those gaps with coaching?

❑ How can I best design my ideal S-Suite, keeping in mind the temperaments that allow my strategic executives to operate from their zone of genius?

❑ How can I best design my ideal T-Suite, keeping in mind the temperaments that allow my tactical executives to operate from their zone of genius?

❑ What roles do I need to adjust on my path to building a Nimble C-Suite composed of my S-Suite and T-Suite?

❑ What are the upgrades to mindset, skillset, toolset, and habitset for each executive that are first required before my executive team can be effective?

Build Your Strategic Map

Create a strategic map of what you want to accomplish and why you want to accomplish it.

Share this strategic map with your executive team and select portions of it to share with your operations team. But keep in mind that, as the responsible executive, you set the direction.

> YOUR BUSINESS ISN'T A PURE DEMOCRACY.
> EMPLOYEES DON'T GET TO VOTE ON STRATEGY.

Build Your Action Plan Sequence

Round up all of the action steps you've identified in this book. Choose a deployment timeline with milestones and KPIs. You can't do everything at once, but you can take your next indicated step right now, and the next one when the time is right, and so forth. This is how you'll start the transformation and stay on track. Count on adjusting on the way; there is no one-size-fits-all plan.

Work with Your Team to Deploy

Your team is the execution engine that makes all of this work. Guide them with your new direction and challenge them to unlearn and relearn these new business models.

Some of them won't make it. Some of them will embrace this new model. Others might wait and see. Cut loose those who resist so the wait-and-see group can more easily pivot from reluctant to supportive.

Tactical deployment is an ever-moving target. You need a flexible team to make your business work well.

> SUCCESS IS NOT A MATTER OF LUCK, IT'S A MATTER OF DISCIPLINE.

Once you design, document, and operate your upgraded business model, you'll have a business with recurring revenue that is sustainable, scalable, profitable, and ultimately saleable, because it is responsive to a transformation economy in which consumers, employees, executives, and vendors choose businesses that are socially responsible.

Sell These Ideas to the Team

When presenting your ideas to your team, this is a sales job: you have to match resources to motivation. This means your ideas must have:

❑ Mission, vision, and brand integrity alignment
❑ Culture and values alignment
❑ Team motivational alignment
❑ Team KPI alignment.

> INVOLUNTARY CHANGE IN THE ABSENCE OF AN EXPLORER MINDSET
> IS ALWAYS PAINFUL.

Any changes to the status quo must show improved performance over the existing team agreement or you're going to have to reset expectations and prepare for a team upheaval. Change, even when voluntary, can feel painful or fearful.

Celebrate Wins, Small and Large

When making changes, celebrating wins maintains motivation because all on the team see progress that helps them value positive change. Let your culture determine how to celebrate. Ask your employees how they'd like to celebrate hitting key goals. They'll probably ask for less than you're willing to fund.

Small wins get small celebrations. Employee of the week and the month goes a long way. Shortening decision cycles gets a celebration. A new major customer gets a celebration.

Large wins get large celebrations. Exceeding targets, competitive wins, new product release, and market recognition get bigger celebrations.

How to Troubleshoot Nimbility Issues

Your first step is to determine if you're facing a systems problem or a people problem. If it's a systems problem, do a deep dive into the execution risk factors we discuss in depth in our companion book, *The Nimble Company*, to identify the root causes.

When troubleshooting people issues, first solve for mindset, next for skillset, and then for toolset. This sequencing is a prime leadership principle.

Now we'll discuss what you'll need to consider, in the psychologically wise order, and a way to illuminate the root causes of the challenges you'll face.

What is Their Maslow's Hierarchy of Needs Level?

You've almost certainly been exposed to Maslow's Hierarchy of Needs. Even though it was first published by Abraham Maslow in 1943 and has been criticized by some academics, we view it as helpful for quickly troubleshooting mindset problems. See Figure 26.

Self-actualization:
problem solving,
morality, spontaneity,
creativity, lack of
prejudice, accepts facts

Esteem: self-esteem, confidence,
achievement, respect of others,
respects others

Love/Belonging: friendship, family,
sexual intimacy

Safety: security of body, of employment, of resources,
of morality, of the family, of health, of property

Physiological: breathing, water, excretion, sleep, food,
homeostasis, sex

Figure 26: Maslow's Hierarchy of Needs Helps Quickly Identify What to Address to Guide a Team Member to Peak Performance

Let's do a quick review of this hierarchy with an eye toward applying it to leadership. Maslow pointed out that our needs on the lower levels of the hierarchy must be substantially met before we can fully access the higher levels.

For example, when a team member is at one of the two lowest levels because of an unmet physiological or psychological need, they won't be able to access higher cognitive functions. At these lower levels, they can only pay attention to the immediate needs of their body or their psyche.

Step one is to check in. How are you doing? How are you feeling? How's the family? Is everything alright? If they've just lost their family pet, been served with divorce papers, worried about a sick relative, etc., they must address this before being able to consider another topic.

Help them any way you can and defer any decisions until they've formulated a plan to resolve these personal life challenges so they can restore life balance. Inspiration to do better doesn't become fully useful until one is within the upper three levels.

An important aspect of Maslow's work: if we get frustrated at a higher level, we'll revert to a lower level. This is likely part of the explanation for why solid performers start to underperform when thwarted.

Nimble Mindset Factors

Next, check in on their mindset factors. The topic of mindset usually centers around a *fixed* mindset or *growth* mindset, as popularized by Carol Dweck's book *Mindset: The New Psychology of Success*. You're about to take that up a notch so you can bring mindset into nimble territory. See Figure 27.

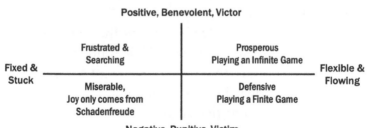

Figure 27: Nimble Mindset Factors — Expected Outcomes (Horizontal Axis) versus Worldview Frame (Vertical Axis) Determines Mindset

The figure's horizontal axis is the fixed versus growth mindset spectrum. We define growth as flexible and flowing. Adding the vertical axis of worldview frame and how they expect the ecosystem to impact their plans, creates a map of what's driving mindset.

You can quickly diagnose their mindset by how they respond to your conversations. Are they frustrated and searching? Are they miserable and only finding joy when others are defeated? Are they defensive and expecting winners and losers? Or do they enjoy a prosperity mindset where we all play to play again?

How to Catalyze Rapid Mindset Shifts

Help them navigate to the prosperous nimble quadrant, where one plays an infinite game. Ed Oakley, co-author of *Enlightened Leadership*[19] shares these questions to help rapidly shift mindset:

❑ *What's going well?* Keep following up their answer with, "What else…" until they run out of answers. This shifts them to a positive view of recent history by reviewing recent wins.

❑ *Why is it going well?* Follow up with, "What else…" until they run out of answers. This rounds up resources, identifies that the environment supports progress, and shows them how they win.

❑ *What do you want to change?* Don't start with this question because without the prior two questions, it becomes a complaint session. With the more positive

---

[19] Ed generously agreed for us to share this with you.

view and resources list, change doesn't look so daunting. Let them choose one suggestion so that it doesn't become overwhelming.

❑ *Why do you want to change this?* This question rounds up the motivation and ultimately the willingness to change.

❑ *What do you see as the path to how we can do this?* This tests to see if they're ready to take the next step and makes them part of the process, a surefire way to garner support for the new destination.

WHAT WE CREATE WE SUPPORT.
– DAN CLARK

Use this simple yet powerful way to help them find their way out of a mindset hole that has trapped them.

Is the Problem Don't Know, Can't Do, or Don't Care?

Next, see if the gap is lack of ability, action, or attitude. Ask yourself, is the problem "don't know," "can't do," or "don't care?" Your gut reaction will be accurate. It may be that two of these issues are getting in the way at the same time.

The solution to ___ is ___:

❑ Don't know – Train and coach them.

❑ Can't do – Get them the tools to do the job or redeploy them where they can do the job.

❑ Don't care – Check on motivation, fix it, move them to where they do care, or enact Collaborative Disengagement (see page 183).

This simple tactic works wonders to troubleshoot and fix people problems.

Get Help from Experts

Our company, NimbilityWorks.com, helps companies like yours become a better version of themselves because your customers want to become a better version of themselves. See more on page 219.

We can help you with this transition. We can be your interim equivalent of a Chief Integrity Officer until you have one in place.

Share Your Story

We can't wait to hear about your journey. Share your story with us. Yes, there will be bumps and bruises; that's part of the voyage of being human and being in business. Without challenge, there is no adventure. Many others will be traveling with you and cheering you on.

Bon Voyage!

Chapter Summary

❑ Create a strategy map that guides you to forming a Nimble C-Suite that includes your S-Suite and T-Suite.
❑ From this map, build an action plan and sequence.
❑ Work with your team to deploy your plan.
❑ When troubleshooting potential deployment issues, start with mindset.

Ask Yourself

❑ Am I willing, able, and ready to become a nimble leader?
❑ Have I made the changes I need to make before I'm personally able to embrace Nimbility?

- ❑ What are my motivations to lead the transformation to a Nimble C-Suite?
- ❑ What happens if I choose to maintain the status quo?
- ❑ What challenges do I foresee leading the Nimble transformation?
- ❑ What is the executive team structure I see as most nimble for my vision and mission?
- ❑ How do my executive team align with the archetypally correct roles?
- ❑ Where are there gaps in my leadership team's capacities? Do I have people who might fill those gaps with coaching?
- ❑ How can I best design my ideal S-Suite, keeping in mind the temperaments that allow my strategic executives to operate from their zone of genius?
- ❑ How can I best design my ideal T-Suite, keeping in mind the temperaments that allow my tactical executives to operate from their zone of genius?
- ❑ What roles do I need to adjust on my path to building a Nimble C-Suite composed of my S-Suite and T-Suite?
- ❑ What are the upgrades to mindset, skillset, toolset, and habitset for each executive that are first required before my executive team can be effective?

Ask Your Team
- ❑ How can you help me facilitate our transition to becoming a Nimble C-Suite?

Action Plan
- ❑ Create a master plan and deployment path for upleveling your C-Suite to Nimbility.

❑ Reach out to NimbilityWorks if you need insight, guidance, or perspective. See page 219 for more information.

❑ Celebrate the successful steps along your path to transforming your team.

❑ Get and read a copy of the companion to this book, *The Nimble Company*, which explores sources and remedies for upheavals, internal & external, avoidable & unavoidable, visible & invisible.

Dedication

We dedicate this book to all the mentors on whose shoulders we stand, and all executives who embrace with all of their minds, hearts, and souls the critical transformation that business must make to realize the better world we all want. You are courageous and we celebrate your heart.

Acknowledgements

We are grateful to our NimbilityWorks cofounders, Mark DiMassimo and Tony Bodoh for their generous, never-ending genius in growing the Nimbility movement.

We recognize and thank the generous, loving people in our life who are our blindspotters and encouragers, sources of inspiration and innovation. In alphabetical order: Sabrina Braham, David Corbin, Mark Hewett, Ed Oakley, Mitch Russo, Chris Stark, Sarah Victory, Rex Wisehart, Bruce Wuollet.

Special thanks for those who provided early input: Mark Hewitt, Douglas Mulhall, and Scott Smith

Mark thanks Molly Smith for her ability to lovingly extract the best of him, even when he resists.

David thanks Laurie Morse for being a magically extraordinary life partner and lightbringer.

And of course, we thank The Divine power that inspired this book and is the Source for much of the content.

This book was outlined and drafted in the inspiring magnificence of Brian Head, UT, and written and edited in peaceful Port St. Joe, FL and shores of San Diego, CA.

About the Authors

Dr. David Gruder, PhD, DCEP, is a clinical and organizational development psychologist, and 12-award-winning bestselling Human Potential Strategist, Business Lifecycle Psychologist, and Culture Architect, who was named America's Integrity Expert by Radio-TV Interview Report.

He has written, contributed to, or been featured, in 25 books, and in Forbes, Inc., Entrepreneur, and Nonprofit Performance magazines, among hundreds of media and podcast interviews. Now in his senior decades, he characterizes himself as a recovering psychologist and professional troublemaker.

David's parents sent him to Woodstock when he was 15 and this experience planted the seeds for his life's mission: to equip leaders and influencers who are called to help repair and evolve the world, with inner, outer and spiritual mindsets and skills to actualize their positive impact.

These days, Dr. Gruder's focus is on catalyzing *Self-Sovereignty That Serves Us All + Governance That Serves Self-Sovereignty*™. He primarily serves Societal Thrival Leaders & Influencers, Middle Market Socially

Responsible Companies, and Integrative Wellbeing Providers, as a trusted advisor, mentor, consultant, trainer, and keynote speaker.

The many hats he currently wears include:

- Integrity Culture Systems™ | Founder and President
- NimbilityWorks™ | Co-Founder & Partner
- NuGen and Lydian Foundation | Co-Founder and Chief Integrity Officer
- Blue Sky Business Resources | Business Lifecycle and M&A Success Psychologist
- Executive Strategy Summits | Executive Development Psychologist
- SynerVision Leadership Foundation™ | Wayfinder, Government Trust Restoration Project Developer, and Principal Trainer
- California Institute for Human Science | Adjunct Faculty
- CEO Space International™ | Legacy Faculty
- ManKind Project | Ritual Elder and Shadow Watcher Training Program Co-Developer and Trainer

He also previously served as Founding President of the Association for Comprehensive Energy Psychology and was an original co-architect and senior trainer for their CEP certification program.

David lives in San Diego, and despite filling all of these roles, he most loves spending plenty of time with his wife Laurie Morse and their two cats.

Also by Dr. David Gruder (Abridged List)

Sensible Self-Help: The First Roadmap for the Healing Journey
The Energy Psychology Desktop Companion

The New IQ: How Integrity Intelligence Serves You, Your Relationships & Our World
The New IQ Workbook: Your Integrity Checkup & Makeover Guide
Conversations With the King: The Enduring Spiritual Legacy of Elvis Presley
Amazing Workplace: Creating the Conditions That Inspire Success (foreword)

And many other publications, training guides, book chapters, forewords, and afterwords.

Website: NimbilityWorks.com and DrGruder.com
LinkedIn: LinkedIn.com/in/Gruder
Twitter: @DavidGruder
Email: Contact@DrGruder.com
Mobile: +1.619.246.1988

Mark S.A. Smith, as a business growth strategist, works with leaders to predictably grow their organization through upgraded executive skills, effective customer acquisition systems, and communication & persuasion strategies.

As an executive coach, executives hire him for strategic coaching, getting unstuck, and use him as a sounding board for developing new, disruptive ideas and choosing new personal and corporate directions.

As co-founder and partner in NimbilityWorks, he brings these skills to clients who must become nimble to thrive in today's chaotic world.

Website: NimbilityWorks.com
LinkedIn: LinkedIn.com/in/MarkSASmith
Twitter: @MarkSASmith
Email: MS@NimbilityWorks.com
Mobile: +1.719.440.0439

Author

Mark wrote seven books and dozens of technology playbooks and sales guides targeting government, educational, healthcare and the private sector and has authored hundreds of articles.

He has also hosted or appeared on hundreds of interviews and podcasts.

Businessman

He has business experience as an electrical engineer, media technologist, computer programmer, hardware salesman, software marketer, and business owner.

Professional Speaker

He speaks at public and corporate events delivering pragmatic ideas to grow and succeed in business. There is no canned speech. He works with you to identify the outcome your group needs and then crafts the presentation to align with your culture, your objectives, and your vision. Contact him for a conversation about speaking at your event.

Builds Business Systems

He designs and implements sales, marketing, and customer acquisition systems that find and recruit willing buyers for disruptive products. He has designed and built channel launch kits, go-to-market playbooks, partner enablement programs, marketing strategy, customer acquisition strategies, executive presentations, systems to up-level business acumen, and more.

Facilitates Executive Strategy Sessions

If you're like many executives in these fast and changing times, you're having challenges clarifying your corporate strategy and getting your executive team all heading the same direction. It's not that your ideas aren't good, the challenge is getting everyone on the same page. Here's a solution.

Using unique, rapid executive decision-making techniques that involve all stakeholders, tapping into the team's personal motivation strategies, and using methods to safely disrupt old ways of thinking, Mark guides your team to get on track and want to stay on track to achieve your goals. And he guarantees it.

Each member of your executive team leaves the event with a "Monday-ready" action plan to deploy with their team to take the correct next steps. You get ongoing support with six months of executive coaching to troubleshoot, encourage, and hold executives accountable for their success.

Mark S.A. Smith facilitates a one and a half to three day on-site executive strategy sessions (timing depends on your mission complexity) with a combination of process training and facilitated conversation about your get-to-market mission.

The deliverables can include:

❑ Discussion of management tools and processes that can be used with your team to accomplish the desired outcome.

❑ Discuss the functions of product, marketing, sales, customer support, operations, finance, and culture in support of the success of this mission.

❑ Discussion of go-to-market processes, selecting the best for your mission based on advanced models.

❑ Clear definition of what success looks like for your mission.

❑ Identify key performance indicators for tracking success and indicating areas which require attention.

❑ Identify resources available to accomplish the mission.

❑ Identify what needs to be accomplished and grounded rationale on doing so.

❑ Identify additional resources required to accomplish the mission.

❑ Create a corporate messaging and communication plan for socializing and inculcating the mission with key team members.

❑ Create a list of prioritized activities and assign responsibility for execution.

Contact NimbilityWorks to discuss if this is right for your team.

Co-Leads the Executive Nimbility Skills Summit

When you can't work any harder, you must work smarter. Specifically created for profit-and-loss-responsible executives of companies, this 2-day event brings executive skills and insights to founders and staff who have been promoted to the executive suite.

What makes this executive event different is the holistic view of business, not just sales or marketing or leadership, but everything required to operate a sustainable, scalable, profitable, and salable business.

Key outcomes:

❑ Develop your executive skill stack — what it is, how it's radically different from a managerial skill stack, and how to intentionally develop it.

❑ Gain a deep understanding of the Seven Business Pillars™: Product, Marketing, Sales, Service, Operations, Finance, and Culture, which give you a holistic view of your business to understand the impact of strategy decisions across pillars.

❑ Master critical executive business concepts that apply to B2B and B2C, for goods and services, for commercial, non-profit, and governmental operations.

❑ Develop your own Monday-ready phased plan to improve results and sustainably and profitably grow your company.
❑ Your satisfaction is guaranteed.

This event is co-led with Dr. David Gruder and other guest speakers. Learn more at NimbilityWorks.com/summit

Also by Mark S.A. Smith (Abridged List)

Guerrilla Trade Show Selling with Jay Conrad Levinson & Orvel Ray Wilson

Guerrilla TeleSelling with Jay Conrad Levinson & Orvel Ray Wilson

Guerrilla Negotiating with Jay Conrad Levinson & Orvel Ray Wilson

Linux in the Boardroom

Security in the Boardroom

From MSP to BSP: Pivot to Profit from I.T. Disruption

And many other custom written books and publications for corporate clients.

About NimbilityWorks

NimbilityWorks brings Nimbility to leaders and their teams with a group of extraordinary experts and authors who have a shared, holistic vision of business development and metamorphosis in times of upheaval.

Our big promise: when we choose to work with you, you will become a market leader in three years or less because of the nimbility skills you and your team will acquire.

The NimbilityWorks team blends many decades of direct experience along with essential processes to illuminate paths for seizing your upheavals. Exactly how we work with you depends on your situation and objectives. We will identify specifics during a conversation with you.

NimbilityWorks brings to courageous leaders of challenged organizations a disruptively holistic perspective, processes, and top-level support so that they can lead productive, profitable upheavals in an era of caution, division, confusion, and extraordinary opportunity.

If this resonates with you, you're the Vision Maker who can lead the direction and culture of your team, and you're looking for at least $10 million in growth this year, schedule a 20-minute conversation with the

NimbilityWorks principals. On the introductory call, you'll be talking with:

❑ Dr. David Gruder: Develop your executive performance and psychological savvy, undo learned helplessness in your team, and master plan how you will harvest blessings from upheavals.

❑ Mark DiMassimo: Make your brand your "unfair" advantage during or because of upheavals. Build and creatively communicate a brand that inspires action with behavior change marketing.

❑ Tony Bodoh: Create a culture realignment around customer expectations, to produce ecstatic, loyal customers.

❑ Mark S A Smith: Rapid facilitation of complex sales and bringing disruptive products & services to market as fast as possible.

These experts are busy, but they've reserved most Tuesday afternoons 2:30 – 3:30 ET for joint conversations with interested executives. Start this process by speaking with one of our team. Book your time with them here => MeetNimbilityWorks.com

NimbilityWorks Team Industry Expertise

Follows is a partial list of the clients that the NimbilityWorks team members have served along with select validations and endorsements, which illustrate the breadth and depth of our team's perspectives.

Agencies, Marketers, Media and Marketing Technology

❑ 5W PR
❑ Boost Engagement
❑ Brave Thinking Institute

- ❑ CNBC
- ❑ CNN.com
- ❑ Forrester Research
- ❑ IPED
- ❑ Reader's Digest
- ❑ Salesforce
- ❑ Shutterstock
- ❑ SmartMoney
- ❑ The Work Institute
- ❑ Trusted Media Brands

"I've worked for some great agencies during my career. I've also hired many others once I made the move to "the client side." All throughout, I've met a handful of creative leaders who don't just talk the talk, but also dig in and make things happen. Mark (DiMassimo) is at the top of the list. He shows up, dives in head first, gets his team(s) to be well-versed in his clients' business, and creates campaigns which truly do inspire action. It's not just his tagline, it's his DNA. Thus far, I've worked with Mark and his team for two different client engagements and can't wait for round III."

– Phillip Sandler, SVP, Head of Marketing & Growth at **Simulmedia**, SVP, Marketing at **Shutterstock**

"David Gruder is a genius, but more than one: he is 8-in-1. His breadth and depth on multiple subjects is unmatched: leadership, culture, program design & development, integrity, systems & process improvements, wordsmithing, and more. Dr. Gruder is an outstanding lens to amplify and accelerate the impact and difference you are out to make."

– Carl Loop, CEO, **Global Business Builders**

"Before spending a day with David, it had been difficult for me to understand or duplicate the special working chemistry that successful teams have. After spending a day in one of his programs, I now have a far better grasp of quality management structures and dynamics. I see how individuals can be helped to share their unique talents and perspectives in ways that co-create productive cultures that are based on collaboration, integrity and trust. I am not only becoming a better executive due to David's insights and facilitation, but a better man.

– V. Tyrone Lam, Chief Operating Officer, **GATC Health**

Education
❑ Alfred University
❑ California Institute for Human Science
❑ Great Minds
❑ Huntington Learning Centers
❑ K-12
❑ San Diego County Office of Education Management Academy
❑ Hocking College
❑ Stride

"Leaders need an integrity check-up and Dr. Gruder is just the man to do it. His simple yet powerful integrity model provides a much-needed shot in the arm."

– Ken Blanchard, Chief Spiritual Officer, **The Ken Blanchard Companies**; Co-author of The One Minute Manager & Leading at a Higher Level

Finance, FinTech, and Financial Media/Education

- ❑ Banker's Healthcare Group
- ❑ CEO Space
- ❑ Citibank
- ❑ Citibank AAdvantage Card
- ❑ Citizens Bank
- ❑ CreditCards.com
- ❑ Everbank/TIAA Bank
- ❑ Forex.com/ Gain Capital
- ❑ IDS/American Express
- ❑ Instinet
- ❑ Investools
- ❑ Online Trading Academy
- ❑ NASDAQ
- ❑ Island ECN
- ❑ MasterCard
- ❑ PMA USA
- ❑ PWC
- ❑ SunTrust
- ❑ TastyTrade
- ❑ ThinkorSwim (now part of TD Ameritrade)
- ❑ TradeStation (Top-Rated Multi-Asset Tech-Forward Brokerage)
- ❑ Voyager (Top Crypto Assets Brokerage App)

"I've always been amazed at Tony's (Bodoh) ability to find creative ways of measuring things and deriving metrics from those measures. He is a constant problem

solver. He has a type of insight I have found very rarely in other people. He's great to work with, as well."
– Peter Mancini, Principal Data Scientist, VP, **Citizens Bank**

"Tony (Bodoh) is able to see beyond the tactical and see the possible. He can help you move from current state to desired state with a clear path for success. Through his deep understanding of customer experience, customer journey, and metrics he provides undeniable value to all organizations he helps."
– Jodi L, Director, Decision Science Analytics, Top-ranked Insurance Company

"Tony Bodoh is a never ending treasure chest of knowledge, experience, awareness and thought leadership. If you are one of the fortunate people to work with Tony or through one of his enterprises, you will come away with a huge increase in all areas of life. He truly cares about his clients and their needs. As one of his clients I give him a resounding 5 star rating. He is an absolute pleasure to work with!"
– Kevin Schultz, District Manager, **PMA USA**

"Tony is one of the most dynamic individuals I have ever had the pleasure to meet and work with. His ability to see multiple sides of any situation gives him the unique perspective to provide some of the most effective solutions I have ever seen. The training and experience Tony has puts him heads and shoulders above even the most prominent figures in his industry. Tony is an asset to whoever is fortunate enough to work with him."

– Michael Bloxton, CEO, **Bloxton Investment Group**

Healthcare and Wellness

- ❑ Association for Integrative Health & Medicine
- ❑ Crunch Fitness
- ❑ New York Health & Racket Club
- ❑ HelloFresh
- ❑ FreshDirect
- ❑ CVS Health
- ❑ Dentistry It's Personal
- ❑ Glaxo Smithkline
- ❑ Holistic Healing Heart Center
- ❑ Holistic Mouth Solutions
- ❑ Ideal Image
- ❑ Memorial Sloan-Kettering Cancer Center
- ❑ National Jewish Health
- ❑ Mt. Sinai
- ❑ Rockland County Hospice
- ❑ Merck
- ❑ Oz Crisis Intervention Center
- ❑ PALM Heath
- ❑ Pfizer
- ❑ Restore
- ❑ Sanoviv Hospital
- ❑ U.S. Naval Hospital, 29 Palms
- ❑ UCSD Medical School
- ❑ Vanderbilt University Medical Center
- ❑ White Plains Hospital
- ❑ WW (Weight Watchers Reinvented)
- ❑ Echelon Fitness

"David Gruder is simply a business decathlete and sales genius with a PhD in psychology, like a superman in a cape. Along the way, he has exceeded all of his promises, and generously taught me what Success requires of me. Engaging Dr. David Gruder has been the best move I've ever made in my career.

– Dr. Felix Liao, DDS, CEO, **Holistic Mouth Solutions**

"Dr. Gruder's work is among the most transformative approaches to business that you will ever see - and he is providing it at a time of the greatest and most uplifting changes in human history."

– Dr. Mark Hewitt, Founder, **NuGen Development** & the **Lydian Foundation**

Franchise/Services
❑ Comcast
❑ Huntington Learning Centers
❑ Jackson Hewitt
❑ Online Trading Academy
❑ Miracle Ear
❑ Ideal Image
❑ Vaco (Recruiting services)

"Mark (DiMassimo) has one of the most brilliant minds in the advertising and branding industry. Working with Mark challenged me to think in new and different ways - - he's always full of ideas that are creative, engaging, and results-oriented."

– Kathy Bell, Sr. Director, Corporate Communications, **Comcast**

"Tony (Bodoh) is one of the most forward thinking people I have ever met. His ideas and philosophies on business and strategy are profound and extremely thought provoking. I can say without a doubt that Tony's successes are directly related to not only his way of approaching an issue or problem, but his drive and determination to find a solution."
— Chris Spintzyk, Director, Technology Solutions, **Vaco**

"Tony (Bodoh) was an out-of-the-box thinker who enjoyed solving big problems, many of which related to helping his Gaylord operations and marketing peers improve performance by interpreting the voices of their guests. This demonstration of value ultimately led to a complete redesign of Gaylord's voice-of-the-guest program architecture, and created a new organizational focus on enabling their operations."
— Matt Cohen, Business Development Manager, **Clarabridge**

Manufacturing
❑ Encompass Group
❑ Fuji
❑ Xtracycle

"Mark (S A Smith) uses a proven process that guides executives to rapidly converge on the best strategy to rapidly grow business. When he facilitated with our team, he was able to help us get to breakthrough results faster than ever. We have clarity and an action plan that will get us to our goals and beyond."

– Greg Snoddy, Vice President Healthcare Sales, **Encompass Group** (Industrial Textiles)

"As a CEO, working with Dr. David Gruder really helped improve my leadership effectiveness. Because I'm now equipped with his 'applied integrity and collaboration' skills in areas like commitment, attention to details, and accountability, I've become able to enjoy holding myself to a higher standard, while also helping those I lead and collaborate with do the same. Dr. Gruder's knowledge, training, insight, and wisdom have helped me immeasurably in operating at the highest level in both my business and personal life. I highly recommend utilizing Dr. Gruder, whether you want the corporation you lead to run at a higher level of peak performance, want to significantly upgrade the quality of your work or personal relationships, or want to create sustainable happiness and fulfillment for yourself."

– Brian Hartley, CEO, **The Body Shield, Inc**.

Nonprofits and NGO

- ❑ ManKind Project
- ❑ Meeting Professionals International
- ❑ National Speakers Association
- ❑ Personal Impact Foundation
- ❑ Society of Government Meeting Planners
- ❑ Soldier for Life
- ❑ SouthCentre, Geneva
- ❑ SynerVision Leadership Foundation
- ❑ USO

"Tony Bodoh is amazing. He helped our company uncover valuable information about our clients. The work he performed was PURE GOLD! I highly recommend Tony Bodoh!"
– John Boggs, CEO, **Brave Thinking Institute**

Real Estate
- Bakerson
- Exit Real Estate Solutions

Tech
- Agilysis
- Apple
- Arrow Electronics
- BEA
- Broadcom
- CDW
- Commvault
- ConnectWise
- Dell
- ePlus
- Gateway
- GAVS
- Hitachi Data Systems
- HP
- IBM
- InfoLink-EXP
- Ingram Micro
- Insight
- Lexmark
- Microsoft

- ❑ NASA
- ❑ NetApp
- ❑ Oracle
- ❑ Raytheon
- ❑ Ruckus
- ❑ Samsung
- ❑ Sanmina
- ❑ Sole Solutions Inc
- ❑ Synnex
- ❑ Tech Data
- ❑ Viavi Solutions

"Dr. Gruder provided a high-performance leadership program to our top leaders at Infolink-exp, and I can say that we were all absolutely thrilled with the level of training we got. What made us decide on his program, as opposed to any other, was the fact that he approaches leadership from a perspective of integrity, which is exactly the underlying value that we want to build our company culture around. The program did not disappoint. Our whole team now has an excellent set of practical tools to improve as individuals, to collaborate with each other, and to perform as leaders. I highly recommend Dr. Gruder's program to anyone wanting to provide their team with the tools needed to make quantum leaps in their ability to collaborate and perform at a high level."
– José A. González, CEO, **Infolink-EXP**

"As we spun out the new company, Viavi Solutions, Mark (S A Smith) was a tremendous partner for our team. He leveraged his practical experience and tools for building trusted customer relationships, but also made the effort to truly understand what we were trying to achieve as we established our new brand. The result was a program that helps us arm our global direct and channel sales team, as well as management in all functions, with a simple way to talk about our new company. The program was not only well-received - it was actually used!"

– Susan Schramm, VP Global Sales, and Channel Effectiveness, **VIAVI Solutions** (Test and Measurement)

"During the time I worked with Mark (S A Smith) I have not seen him turn away a challenge. He is one of the most creative business solution-oriented professionals I have met. His ability to quickly understand, analyze and turn problems into executable solutions is well-founded in the experience and personality he brings to the job. I recommend Mark highly to anybody looking for solid business solutions."

– Rene Neumann, Program Director, Global Distributed Channel Management, **IBM**

Travel, Leisure, and Hospitality
- Avis Budget Group, Budget Rent-a-Car
- Garza Blanca Residence Club
- Gaylord Hotels
- Gaylord Springs Golf Links
- Grand Ole Opry
- Gulf Shores & Orange Beach CVB
- Marriott
- Quicken Loans Arena
- Ryman Auditorium

- ❑ Starwood Preferred Guest
- ❑ American Airlines AAdvantage Program
- ❑ Tafer Hotels and Resorts
- ❑ The Plaza Hotel
- ❑ Millennium Hotels
- ❑ Starwood
- ❑ Wildhorse Saloon
- ❑ Wyndham Garden

"Tony is a master at taking complex situations and breaking them down into manageable components that can easily be made actionable and shared. His communication skills at all levels of the organization are effective and impactful. I wish I had a dozen Tony's on my team!"

– Arthur Keith, General Manager, **Gaylord Opryland Hotel and Convention Center**

"Mark (DiMassimo) has this unique ability to take an award-winning concept from the initial phase to the execution embracing all whom he is working with along the journey as key contributors and stakeholders. He is as generous as he is inspiring. ...Mark has always been instantly available to me by phone, email or text, whenever the need arises for assistance, even knowing that taking my call would have no personal direct benefit. And I didn't even mention his results – top of our class, Platinum Award, and phenomenal growth – and we did it all with ideas and creativity. Marketing Magician!"

– Tom Civitano, Former Director of Sales and Marketing at **The Plaza Hotel**, currently Director of Sales & Marketing at **Stamford Marriott Hotel & Spa**